SPIRITUAL ENTERPRISE

SPIRITUAL ENTERPRISE

Doing Virtuous Business

Theodore Roosevelt Malloch

ENCOUNTER BOOKS
New York and London

First edition published in 2008 by Encounter Books, an activity of Encounter for Culture and Education, Inc., a nonprofit, tax exempt corporation.

Encounter Books website address: www.encounterbooks.com

Text design and composition by Wesley B. Tanner / Passim Editions, Ann Arbor.

Manufactured in the United States and printed on acid-free paper.

⊗ The paper used in this publication meets the minimum requirements of ANSI/NISO Z39.48-1992 (R 1997) (Permanence of Paper).

FIRST EDITION

Library of Congress Cataloging-in-Publication Data

Malloch, Theodore R.
  Spiritual enterprise : doing virtuous business / Theodore Roosevelt Malloch.
    p. cm.
  Includes bibliographical references and index.
  ISBN-13: 978-1-59403-222-6 (hbk. : alk. paper)
  ISBN-10: 1-59403-222-X (hbk. : alk. paper) 1. Business—Religious aspects. I. Title.
  HF5388.M29 2008
  261.8'5—dc22   *2008001920*

FOR

Sir John Marks Templeton

AND ALL WHO HUMBLY SEEK TRUTH

AND GREATER SPIRITUAL INSIGHT

Self-discipline, a sense of justice, honesty, fairness, chivalry,

moderation, public spirit, respect for human dignity, firm

ethical norms — all of these are things which people must

possess before they go to market and compete with each

other. These are the indispensable supports which preserve

both market and competition from degeneration. Family,

church, genuine communities, and tradition are their

sources.

Wilhelm Röpke,
A Humane Economy, 1957

Contents

 *Foreword*

I N BIBLICAL TIMES, the right of private property mattered to people. If it hadn't, the commandment "Thou shalt not steal" would
not have made any sense. There were many lively markets in that
era, and Jerusalem itself was a critically important marketplace at
the crossroads of three continents. There was also plenty of private
profit to be made; the Bible is full of stories about such profit, and it
was with gifts contributed from these profits that the great and beautiful Temple of Solomon was built. Private property, markets and
profits are all fundamental components of traditional economies,
not just of the relatively new and distinctive economy we know as
capitalism.

Capitalism, to define it in its essence, is creative, sensible and intellectual action taken in the service of enterprise. And enterprise is the
act of noticing, discovering, and inventing new possibilities before
anyone else does. What makes capitalism so dynamic is its source in
this powerful, innovating habit of mind, as well as its focus on a host
of practical and empowering activities and institutions.

In ancient and medieval times, wealth typically arose from the
ownership of great estates, vineyards and orchards, or from generous
rewards for government service. But at the dawn of the capitalist era,
the source of wealth began to shift from ownership of land to posses-
sion of creative insights—the clear discovery of new and better products, or of superior processes for producing and distributing them,
or of new services never before provided. As capitalism took hold, its
fundamental reality became a spiritual reality, one whose vital core is

fruitful, generative insights. When Ronald Reagan became president of the United States in 1981, personal computers, mobile telephones and the Internet were unknown to the world's consumers, and many of what have become the largest industries in the world did not even exist. Immense fortunes were made from these new discoveries, and Bill Gates became the wealthiest man in the world specifically because of his patents and copyrights, that is, his ownership of ideas.

Even money—filthy mammon, which used to be regarded as such a thoroughly material thing—draws its real value from qualities that belong more to the human spirit than to merely material realities. When people lose confidence in governments and in their currencies, money becomes relatively valueless. Think of Germany during the Weimar period, when people needed wheelbarrows full of currency to buy a loaf of bread. Who would have guessed that political faith and confidence were of more weight than solid, tangible money? Yet throughout history they have often proven to be so.

Prior to the introduction of capitalism, popular wisdom as well as the Bible held that "the poor ye shall always have with you." The perennial existence of large majorities of desperately poor people wasn't viewed as immoral, but rather as a simple fact of life. No one worked diligently to alter that reality; no one thought of it as a tragedy or a scandal. Yet the introduction of capitalist economies into world history slowly began to revolutionize the moral order. As Hannah Arendt notes in her wonderful book *On Revolution*, Europeans began to take note of a new experiment under way in North America, one that, within a generation or two, allowed hundreds of thousands of formerly poor people to live in comfortable homes of their own and enjoy unprecedented prosperity in a place where a virtually universal emergence from poverty was taken for granted. This novel and utterly astonishing reality shocked the conscience of Europe and created, Arendt argues, *die soziale Frage*, the crisis of conscience out of which grew socialism and communism, and other movements of vast social reform.

It was Adam Smith who, in 1776, asked the most important of revolutionary questions. His question wasn't "What is the cause of poverty?"—which, if correctly answered, could have led only to the discovery of how to create more poverty. Instead, Smith asked a question that had been overlooked by Descartes, Thomas Aquinas, Aristotle and every other great thinker before him: "What is the nature and the cause of the wealth of nations?" Smith was the first person in history to conceive of a world from which poverty could be banished, a world of "universal affluence" in which every woman, man and child would be liberated from the prison of poverty. That was his goal. It was a remarkably altruistic dream, and it is a vision that, from his day to this, has been the universal mission of capitalism as well.

Consider this: A great economic miracle has been under way on the mainland of Asia in the years since 1980. The giant economies of China and India have rather dramatically turned towards capitalist economic methods and have released the dynamism of individual enterprise, initiative and creativity among peasants and city dwellers alike. In this process, China and India have raised more than a half billion people out of poverty within the span of only thirty years. Never before have so many people emerged out of hopeless lives in so short a time.

As Jagdish Bhagwati notes in his brilliant book *In Defense of Globalization,* the enormous creative potential of global capitalism can best be observed by comparing the trajectories of Africa and Asia over the last quarter century. In 1970, a full 76 percent of the world's poor were in Asia, while only 11 percent were in Africa. By 1998, however, China and India had lifted so many people out of poverty that those percentages had nearly reversed themselves. Asia now is home to 15 percent of the world's poor, while Africa is home to 66 percent.

This astonishing development in two of the world's most important nations vividly demonstrates that new, job-creating businesses—most of them small businesses—are the key strategic institutions in the morally vital pursuit of social justice. Job-creating businesses are not just the best, but the only hope of the poor. Businesses small and large are also the best hope of a civil society; they alone generate the private funds that allow voluntary associations to serve the needs of the disenfranchised.

Businesses similarly are the world's best hope for democracy. If democracy gave people the opportunity to vote for their leaders regularly but offered them no chance to improve their economic condition, they would find democracy very hard to love. What people rightly love best about democracy is the economic opportunity and prosperity it can bring them. It is democratic capitalism, not merely democracy, that they understand to be worthy of their devotion, energy and practice.

Capitalism demands transparency and honest accounting and reporting. It insists on the rule of law and the strict observance of contracts. It demands hard work, inventiveness, initiative and a spirit of responsibility and respect. It teaches the patient acceptance of small gains, and it proves the value of steady and insistent progress. During the nineteenth century, Great Britain achieved an average annual growth rate of 1.5 percent of its gross domestic product, with the astonishing result that the average income of the ordinary laborer in Britain quadrupled in a single century. The moral habits of invention, discovery, hard work, persistence, saving and investment brought about the greatest improvement in the condition of the poor—including advances in hygiene, medicine, longevity, and physical and emotional well-being—in all of recorded history.

Capitalism carries in its wake the potential for immense transformation, a true and permanent change that is moral in nature. Those nations, peoples and businesses who neglect the moral ecology of their own cultures cannot enjoy the fruits of such transformation, and capitalism must be essentially moral or it falters, declines and fails. Spiritual enterprise, as this insightful and eloquent book suggests, is capitalism in its most profound and important form.

Michael Novak

Olin Senior Fellow,
American Enterprise Institute

Introduction: Spiritual Entrepreneurship

For years, I've paid close attention to something that fascinates me—the ability of people with religious faith and spiritual commitment to make great successes of their businesses. Success comes to them, I believe, because faith changes business for the better, just as it changes lives. It injects into business something that I call "spiritual capital." Agnostics and nonbelievers make use of spiritual capital as well, but only people of faith renew it. And by replenishing spiritual capital, they benefit us all.

The recent downfalls of WorldCom, Enron, Adelphia, Tyco and other once high-flying companies have flooded newspapers, television screens and courtrooms around the country with important, and often difficult, questions about the ethics of business—or the consequences of their troubling absence. From inventors to investors, venture capitalists to investment bankers, and employees to managers, people inside America's businesses are all too aware of the need for better corporate governance, for more accountability and transparency.

But from what source do the virtues that inform ethical behavior arise? And why are they so essential to the modern economy we have come to depend on for our creative freedom and our prosperity? Many people have real anxiety about virtue—particularly as it pertains to business—because it's a concept that is increasingly absent from our public vocabulary. Today, the general public holds corporate CEOs in lower esteem than at any time in history, ranking them below lawyers and politicians. Because of the crimes and scandals perpetrated by many of those company officials, people are rightly disillusioned, even disgusted, by what they glimpse of corporate America's goals and the nefarious means with which it seeks to achieve them.

I strongly believe that profit-*only* companies are, in fact, parasitic, and that they damage the economy at large with their limited and self-focused view of their role in the marketplace. But companies that commit themselves to a more holistic core mission and are steeped in spiritual capital often succeed in righting wrongs and creating genuine personal and social progress, while also succeeding in generating strong profits. The moral outrage that people feel in response to the past decade of scandal and deceit is entirely legitimate, and it leads to compelling questions about the true purpose of business and the virtues that are necessary to sustain it and a free economy.

The vital link between an unfettered economy and spiritual life has long been an important subject in the social and economic sciences. In his groundbreaking 1921 book, *The Protestant Ethic and the Spirit of Capitalism*, Max Weber, often acknowledged as the father of modern sociology, argues that the rise of capitalism can be explained only as a byproduct of Protestant, and specifically Calvinist, ethics. The Protestant emphasis on individual accountability to God reinforces a spirit of honest dealing and attention to moral behavior, Weber believed. Yet his thesis is no longer entirely credible—not because there is no connection between capitalism and the Protestant ethic, but because the connection is both wider and deeper than he understood. Capitalism thrives not because of its relationship to Protestantism, but because of its profound connection to a fundamentally religious frame of mind. In a series of books that culminate with *Pyramids of Sacrifice*, published in 1974, Peter Berger argues that religious values are critically important in creating the trust and entrepreneurship that a free economy requires, and that the creation of wealth, when properly understood, is a spiritual exercise with a deeply theological meaning and far from simply an expression of "materialist" values.

Berger writes from a Protestant perspective, but his thoughts are echoed by the Catholic theologian and philosopher Michael Novak, whose foreword opens this book and who, in *Business as a Calling*, demonstrates how the Catholic theological tradition doesn't simply *condone* business, but instead views it as a vocation by which we have the opportunity to fulfill our duties to God and our fellow human beings. Novak describes the capitalist economy—together with democracy and the rule of law—as the foundational components of a comprehensive social enterprise. Together, they create the conditions in which individual initiative is released and the creative potential of each member of society is given the opportunity to find fulfillment.

*

In societies both advanced and primitive, there are only three possible models for the way in which wealth is created. In the first, wealth is essentially mysterious, guarded by spirits or gods who only reluctantly offer it to mortals—who, in turn, are forced to employ magic and trickery if they hope to obtain it. In the second model, wealth is acquired by tribal, corporate or national conquests that simply seize it from others. This notion presumes that wealth is a fixed resource and that if one person makes money, then necessarily another loses it. A third model—the one to which I enthusiastically subscribe—is the idea that wealth can be created, and that it is most successfully created when we employ skills and talents given to us by God.

Capitalism—just another name for the free economy—is a system in which capital is held in private hands, and in which people are free to spend it, waste it, invest it, accumulate it, and share it as they choose. In the nearly century-long contest between capitalism and communism, capitalism triumphed. This was neither because capitalism is more efficient, although it is, nor because it leads to a fairer distribution of wealth, although it does that as well. Capitalism was able to prove its superiority because it alone expresses and preserves the gift of human freedom.

In a free economy, people give freely of their energies, talents and knowledge because they wish the best for themselves, their families and others. And at the same time—as if "by an invisible hand," as Adam Smith famously put it—they also perform a vital service for the economy as a whole, freely generating productivity, something that inevitably dwindles when people are coerced into maintaining it.

A free economy sustains itself by generating the momentum that enables individuals to make rational use of their powers. In a free market, for example, price is a reliable guide to the utility and scarcity of goods, wages a reliable guide to the value of a skill, and profit a reliable sign that a product or service is socially useful. In a free economy, individuals can make the best use of their talents, skills and experience, make money and spend it—all in ways they believe will bring them the most reward. They are motivated to do what they believe is best for themselves, and in doing so they benefit others to whom they are bound in a network of mutual competition and support.

"Nonsense," say the critics of capitalism. There is more to life than money, and "getting and spending, we lay waste our powers," as Wordsworth put it. From this negative perspective, the capitalist market situates the profit motive at the very center of life, and so corrodes what ought to occupy that privileged place—morality, loyalty, charity and spirituality. Capitalism and corporations are the enemy of the moral life, these critics argue, and the recipe for a heartless society. From every corner, the critics of capitalism accuse those who actually create wealth of greed and plunder, of being self-obsessed and selfish.

In this book, I answer that criticism, exploring a notion that has largely escaped the attention of both critics and defenders of the free market, yet which is absolutely fundamental to the vitality of a capitalist economy and the success and happiness of those who engage in it—that is, the bold idea that the creation of wealth by *virtuous* means is the most important thing we can do for ourselves and others, for our society and for the world at large.

We create wealth by producing what others find useful. And we do this by investing our talents and hoping that ultimately they are rewarded, just as Jesus described in the parable he told two millennia ago. The critical factor in producing wealth is not land or toil or machinery. It is entrepreneurship: the imagining, creating and running of an enterprise. This cannot be done without risk, and the successful entrepreneur is one who knows how to take risks, assume responsibility for their outcome, and act responsibly towards those whom he includes in his gamble. *That* is how wealth is created. By creating wealth, we use God's gifts responsibly; and provided that we work towards that goal in a spirit of humility and gratitude, we benefit all those with whom we deal along the way.

On the other hand, those who create wealth for the purpose of using it to dominate others, and who see wealth simply as an amplification of personal power, are parasites on the free economy, and they add nothing to our collective well-being. Wealth creation in its truest form is a collective process, one in which people freely pool their energies and resources. They do so because they comfortably rely on their shared moral values as they work to achieve shared goals.

Humility and gratitude are not just ways in which people acknowledge their Creator, nor are they merely gestures designed to elicit sympathy in others. They are deep-seated virtues whose purpose is to direct our activity towards the common good and to help release our best creative energies. These virtues are critically important components of what I call spiritual capital, and much of this book is devoted to exploring how they arise, how they function, and what they contribute to a successful business.

People who take their faith seriously regard themselves as stewards of the resources entrusted to them, and also as stewards of their own potential. They do not see their presence on earth as a mere accident, one without meaning or explanation in transcendental terms. Instead, people of faith recognize that they live for a purpose, and that they must give proof of their worth to their Creator. For them, freedom of choice is not a narrow or legally circumscribed idea, but rather the very essence of human life, inviting us all to choose at every point between right and wrong, good and evil, the godly and the godless way of doing things. Freedom of choice is not just an array of possibilities. Instead, it is a profound kind of self-expression, one in which you exercise your God-given faculties to the best of your ability, and in which you are guided by the virtues we collectively hold dear. Far from restricting business success, faith dramatically amplifies our economic potential and enables the free market to create wealth for us all, benefiting everyone. Virtuous enterprise accomplishes two enormously important things: it makes the world in which we live a better place, and it makes our businesses far more successful, more *profitable* than they otherwise would be.

I write as a committed Christian, but what I say does not reflect a narrow or specifically sectarian Christian theology. Throughout the book, I draw examples of virtue and spiritual enterprise from other faiths, and I heartily believe that spiritual enterprise is often conducted from Jewish, Muslim, Hindu, Buddhist and other perspectives, and that every religion and spiritual tradition offers blueprints for building spiritual capital in its own distinctive way.

Almost certainly, there is no single set of religious principles that regulates a given economic system. Instead, regardless of their faith community, all spiritual people make individual and collective choices in which personal faith is a decisive factor. Individuals are motivated by their faith to take note of others and their needs, to regard themselves as objects of judgment, and to conduct their personal and business lives in a spirit of accountability, both to God and to their fellow human beings.

It is important to emphasize that what is true of the virtuous creation of wealth in developed countries is also true in underdeveloped countries. The entrepreneur is as essential in what used to be called the Third World as he or she is in the developed world. Those moral and spiritual assets that make enterprise possible are as critically important in Africa today as they remain in Europe and North America. Economies stagnate, decline or fail not merely for lack of material or monetary investment, but also—and I believe more importantly—because of overwhelming obstacles to the spirit of enterprise.

Development requires economic growth; in turn, growth requires the catalytic drive of the entrepreneur, and entrepreneurship exists only where freedom of action is combined with personal responsibility. In all its myriad forms, accountability is a spiritual asset that is forged by the faith that inspires and governs it, and it does not easily come into being in other ways.

Wherever faith dynamically arises, you see hope, too, swelling in its wake, just as you can currently witness this dynamism in Indonesia, in offshore Chinese communities, in the now burgeoning economy of India, and even in the Latin American evangelical communities that are creating islands of free commerce despite strict, and often corrupt, state control. Human beings, guided by faith and hope, add value to nature and transform it in powerfully positive ways. Without faith or hope, humankind simply exploits the natural world and leaves it weakened, threatened and very much at risk.

The creation of wealth requires capital investment, and I believe the most essential part of that investment is the spiritual capital with which enterprise begins, then flowers and bears fruit—talents creating and sustaining still more talents, and all of us thriving in a vital spiritual bond.

SPIRITUAL ENTERPRISE

1. Spiritual Capital

Grace is given of God but knowledge is bought in the market.

Arthur Clough

B UILT TO LAST, a classic study of "visionary companies," reveals an interesting discovery: the company that succeeds in circumstances whereits rivals falter or go the wall is not the kind of "profit machine" envisaged by the opponents of corporate capitalism. On the contrary, although it aims to be profitable, the visionary company understands profit in the way that a biologist understands oxygen—not the goal of life, but the thing without which there is no life. A corporation may be motivated by an ideology of group membership, low prices and consumer satisfaction, like Wal-Mart; or it may be fired by a desire to make a real contribution to society, like Hewlett-Packard (HP). It may even impress upon the world and its workforce that its primary purpose is to honor God (as in the case of Dacor, which I discuss in Chapter Three). The point is that, however the company describes its motivating principles, profit does not appear as the goal, but as the side effect of pursuing those principles.

In this connection it is worth quoting the words of John Young, CEO of HP from 1976 to 1992:

> Maximizing shareholder wealth has always been way down the list. Yes, profit is a cornerstone of what we do—it is a measure of our contribution and a means of self-financed growth—but it has never been the *point* in and of itself. The point, in fact, is to *win*, and winning is judged in the eyes of the customer and by doing something you can be proud of. There is symmetry of logic in this. If we provide real satisfaction to real customers, we will be profitable.

What Young is saying is clear: by aiming exclusively at profit, you risk losing your sense of purpose; by pursuing your sense of purpose, on the other hand, you gain profit as through an invisible hand. Moral and economic values are not in competition; in the right context, to pursue the one is to obtain the other. Moreover, as *Built to Last* shows through the telling contrast between HP and Texas Instruments, the firm that puts profit at the top of its agenda, making all else subordinate, very soon begins to lose its competitive edge.

A team of researchers has shown the close connection, in particular cases, between moral conviction and business success. Through the exercise of "moral imagination," a firm can further the moral goals of its members, providing them with the personal satisfaction that comes from doing good, without sacrificing profitability. Some go further, suggesting a kind of secular basis for the moral dimension of business, as people enter through business into moral relations with their fellows, and work comes to function as the foundation of social harmony, imbuing life with purpose—performing the role that religion once performed. These studies take us far along the road to understanding the moral basis of capitalism and the resources of social capital on which it draws. But they do not go far enough. There is another and deeper root of business success, and that is what I explore in this book.

Social Capital

For close on a century, sociologists, economists and political scientists in the academy have been developing the concept of "social capital," drawing on the language of economics in order to describe the accumulated social resources inherited by each new generation from its predecessor. These resources are used in managing the day-to-day affairs of social existence, and they include customs, language, manners and morals—in short, all the practices that are taught to us by our parents in order to make us fit members of society. These things cannot be invented anew by each generation, since they are the distillation of a long process of accommodation. As many since Tocqueville have shown, the rules, customs and traditions that enable people to live together in a great society are also products of the "invisible hand." They are the beneficial results of cooperation and competition between neighbors, and the spontaneous byproducts of their attempts to live in peace. The very same freedom that produces the capitalist economy also produces the social capital that is needed if it is to run successfully.

The World Bank defines social capital as "the norms and social relations embedded in social structures that enable people to coordinate action to achieve desired goals." Robert Putnam, a Harvard political scientist who has made social capital into his specialty, describes it similarly: " 'social capital' refers to features of social organizations such as networks, norms, and social trust that facilitate coordination and cooperation for mutual benefit." His landmark 1993 book, *Making Democracy Work*, convincingly demonstrated the political, institutional and economic value of social capital. In *Bowling Alone*, he presented a scholarly and provocative account of America's declining social capital. Numerous comparative economic studies by the World Bank and the United Nations corroborate Putnam's thinking: some regions of the globe lag behind while others thrive due to their social capital.

A recent study examines the role that social capital invested in a company plays in economic success. *In Good Company* describes social capital as the "stock of active connections among people, the trust, mutual understanding, and shared values and behaviors that bind members of human networks and communities and make cooperative action possible." Social capital involves the social elements that contribute to knowledge sharing, innovation and productivity. It makes any organization or cooperative group into something more than a collection of individuals intent on achieving their own private purposes. This social capital, it turns out, is so integral to business life that without it, corporate action—and consequently productive work—is not possible.

Like economic capital, social capital can be accumulated and invested. It is built through creating networks of trust and goodwill, which enable people spontaneously to pool their intellectual and physical resources in a common enterprise. A seminal work titled *Trust: The Social Virtues and the Creation of Prosperity* argues that communities with a culture of trust and accountability are able to prosper in adverse circumstances and to create wealth seemingly *ex nihilo*. Hong Kong, a tiny peninsula without natural resources, and with some 5 percent of China's population, has regularly accounted for 30 percent of the Chinese GNP. The difference between Hong Kong and mainland China (which has every possible natural resource) lies in the culture of trust that was protected under British administration in Hong Kong, but systematically destroyed by the communists on the mainland.

Western societies have built up a great stock of social capital in the form of culture, networks, institutions and laws. In each area of human endeavor they have added to this stock, accumulating works of art and music, games and sports, festivals and competitions, through which individuals rehearse their social feelings and refresh their commitments. Social capital can be wisely invested, as when we found a school or university and endow it with good teachers, good books and good facilities, so helping the fund of knowledge and skills to grow. It can dwindle, as many researchers have shown, through the gradual retreat from social contact. It can also be wasted, and the conspicuous waste of social capital is one of the most unhappy features of our societies today. This waste has been documented by several authors who have shown the way in which, by throwing economic resources into the welfare system, we do not merely waste those resources, we also waste social capital—producing the welfare-dependency that prevents people from learning how to be on equal and responsible terms with others, subsidizing indolence and exhausting our teachers, social workers and doctors with the thankless task of caring for people who are often unwilling to care for themselves.

Some critics of the welfare system have become highly controversial on account of the challenge they present to liberal orthodoxies. We are heirs to a long tradition of free discussion and open dialogue; we solve our problems by discussing them and attempting to discover their causes and cures. The many institutions devoted to free discussion that we have built over time represent an important accumulation of social capital. Universities, newspapers, academic journals, House and Senate committees—all these are invaluable assets in which we have distilled the precious habit of free opinion, in order to invest our thinking in the collective process of social and political reform. For a variety of reasons, however, it can no longer be assumed that a university will permit the free discussion of those questions that are most in need of a solution. Academic leaders have been driven to resign following remarks that, although true, ran contrary to feminist orthodoxy or political correctness; and these cases illustrate the enormous cultural shift that has occurred in American universities. Where once there was a culture of free enquiry, there is now a culture of radical indoctrination. Integrity and educational vision have taken a back seat to ideology. In this and similar ways, the accumulated capital of scholarship goes to waste. This capital can be squandered and, in time, lost.

Of course, the truth has a way of making itself known, even in times when there is a penalty for expressing it. Still, we should not be complacent. We should recognize that much of our social capital in Western societies is being squandered, and that we need a far better understanding of its value if we are to invest it as we should. Nor should we ignore the reason for this waste of vital resources. The left-liberal orthodoxies of the universities and the welfare culture both belong to the same anticapitalist frame of mind that sees success in business as a proof of "greed," which imagines wealth creation to be a zero-sum game, and which blames capitalism and the free economy for the plight of the world's impoverished nations and marginalized groups. These attitudes are, I believe, profoundly mistaken. But they are so widespread, and so immune to refutation among those infected by them, that we shall need to explain just why they have arisen and why they persist.

Wise investment means responsible investment, with social capital just as much as monetary capital. And investment is responsible only if someone is accountable for it, in the way that a board of directors is accountable to its shareholders or an elected politician to his constituents. Too much social capital now passes through the hands of unaccountable bureaucrats. Those who run our state education system can evade all penalties for the loss of knowledge as the curriculum is degraded and dumbed down; for the loss of moral standards as sex education is diverted from its true goal of teaching restraint to the false goal of teaching options; for the loss of manners and discipline in the young, who need these things every bit as much as their parents needed them, but who are being deprived of the legacy from which a successful life in society can begin.

In short, social capital is like economic capital in that it is easier to lose than to gain, and easier to spend on instant gratification than on the long-term benefits for which it is designed. By thinking of our social inheritance on the analogy of economic capital, we learn to safeguard and build on it, and we become wary of the ways in which it can be squandered and destroyed. And one of the most creative ways in which we build on social capital is through free enterprise, pursued as a calling.

Social Capital and the Market

The free economy is not the enemy but the friend of social capital. The free economy is an accountable economy, in which the cost of risk falls on the one who takes it, and in which reward comes to those who pay their debts and who deal openly and justly with their fellows. As we know from the law of contract, actors in a free economy are duty-bound to keep agreements and to compensate those whom they wrong by any breach. This is just one way in which the free economy encourages important virtues—notably honesty and accountability, and the ability to accept the cost of risk-taking. These virtues are a fundamental part of social capital. We teach them to our children, and we deplore their absence in the cheats and sneaks who hide in the crevices of the modern economy—and nowhere more than in its vast bureaucracies.

Advocates of state intervention tell another story. The market, they say, erodes human virtues by putting selfishness ahead of compassion. They view the private sector and free markets as morally corruptible, being sources of commercialism, materialism and individualism. Since the power of a central government is needed to bend society towards their ideal, those on the left favor always increasing the power of government over the private sector, and see the distribution of economic resources through the agency of government as the way to change the direction of trade from private profit to "the spiritual self-perfection of man," to use Isaiah Berlin's phrase. In this way, the moral critique of the free economy leads imperceptibly and of its own accord to the advocacy of state control, which in turn means control by bureaucrats. Put another way: by despising the profit motive, we insensibly move towards a situation in which those who take the risks are controlled by others who take no risks at all, and whose costs are covered at every juncture by the all-providing state. To think of this as a moral improvement is to lose sight of the true role of morality—forming character, instilling responsibility, and thereby establishing the dignity and happiness of the person and of the communities that people create and sustain.

There is another tradition that sees the free economy as an integral part of the moral life, underpinning virtues and also depending upon them. As Adam Smith made clear, the free economy that is advocated in *The Wealth of Nations* depends at every point on the rational sympathies that he describes so movingly in *The Theory of Moral Sentiments*. The idea of a conflict between the "selfish" world of free markets and the "benevolent" world of human sympathy is a myth. The two worlds flourish together and depend upon the same input of moral virtues if they are to provide their benefits. And the relation between virtue and the free economy is reciprocal. A free market depends upon honesty and accountability; it also tends to produce these virtues. People can succeed in the short term through cheating and confidence tricks, but the market soon exposes them, as it exposed the directors of Enron. Long-term success depends upon trust, and people trust only those who have shown themselves to be honest, accountable, fair-dealing and willing to accept the cost of their own risk-taking.

That is why the theory of economic capital and the theory of social capital are not two theories but one. They describe two necessary inputs into the modern economy—two indispensable resources from which a healthy and prosperous economy can grow, and a healthy and prosperous community can take charge of its own future.

Spiritual Capital

The idea of capital accumulation and investment can be used to describe other and equally important inputs into a flourishing economy. The term "human capital" first appeared in 1961 in an *American Economic Review* article, "Investment in Human Capital," by a Nobel Prize–winning economist. Since then, economists have loaded much baggage onto the concept, but most agree that skills, experience and knowledge, embodied in human beings, are a species of capital that plays an indispensable part in the generation of profit. Some add personality, appearance, reputation and credentials to the mix. Still other management gurus equate human capital with its owners, suggesting that it consists of "skilled and educated people." *Human Capital: What It Is and Why People Invest It* demonstrates through examples the many ways in which the skills, experience and virtues of the employee constitute a real and profitable asset of the firm. Indeed, it has become almost trite to mention that the most important assets in both economic development and firm behavior are the human assets. The old division of the "factors of production" into land, labor and capital now has a decidedly antiquated air. Labor has been absorbed into "human capital," and land is just one among the many raw materials that this capital transforms.

But there is another application of the capital concept that is still too often overlooked, and which underpins all that people have noticed in the subtle functioning of human capital: namely spiritual capital, the subject of this book. Two Nobel laureate economists have used the term "spiritual capital" in their writings, referring to the aspect of capital that is linked to our spiritual life. I aim to make the meaning more precise by showing exactly what spiritual capital amounts to in practice. For the moment we may define it as the fund of beliefs, examples and commitments that are transmitted from generation to generation through a religious tradition, and which attach people to the transcendental source of human happiness. Let me give you two historical examples to illustrate what this means.

In 1807, after decades of diligent legislative and business persuasion, William Wilberforce, member of the British Parliament, finally succeeded with much difficulty in putting an end to the slave trade. The abolition of slavery itself came decades later, but Wilberforce's stirring actions set it in motion. What motivated him and the Clapham sect of followers around him was an almost evangelical faith in the dignity of man as made in the image of God. Using the spiritual capital built over centuries of faith led to one of the greatest and most important business-economic actions in Western history.

Fast-forward to the middle of the twentieth century and the heartland of America, to a Dutch community on the shores of Lake Michigan. There a brilliant CEO was busy articulating a set of business practices called values-based leadership, which led to an entirely new and deeply spiritual way of conducting business. He founded a company that was no mom-and-pop store; it became a Fortune 500 giant with sales well over a billion dollars. The CEO of Herman Miller, which manufactures office furniture, was Max DePree, formerly a college and seminary president and an author of some acclaim.

DePree's vision was based on his Reformed theological understanding of man, freedom and economics. In deceptively simple language he described a spiritual approach to leadership in the corporation, which he put into practice over his entire tenure in the business. Leaders at every level, he said, are responsible for the assets they command. The artful leader recognizes human diversity and makes full use of employees' gifts and talents. DePree forcefully argued for and practiced a management of persuasion, democratic participation, covenantal relationships and teamwork, resting on shared purpose, dignity and choice. In fact, he often compared leadership in a business setting to the art of leading a jazz ensemble.

Economists, who are too often divorced from real-life experience in the economy, are especially tempted to adopt a simple model of the human being as a creature driven by cost and benefit. This model of the person has come down to us from Hobbes and Mandeville; it inspired the utilitarian morality of Bentham and his followers, and is presupposed by countless textbooks of neoclassical economics. *Homo economicus*, however, does not exist and never has existed. He is a convenient abstraction from the real complexities of human life. Adam Smith saw this clearly and did not fail to consider the moral preconditions of the market economy: the sentiments of sympathy, benevolence and compassion, of approval, disapproval and indignation, which underpin the social order and make it possible to engage in business in the first place. Human beings are not just profit-maximizers. They have moral scruples, personal commitments and the desire for happiness. These set limits to their plans for personal profit, and also stimulate them to pursue profit in ways that honor their higher values.

A cynic would respond that these moral constraints on the profit motive mean that the winnings go to the immoralist. The one without scruples and commitments, who can bypass the barriers to self-seeking that impede more timorous people, will be the one who succeeds in the market. This, in essence, is the view of the left-liberal orthodoxy that prevails in so many Western institutions. But it is the opposite of the truth, as shown in *The Moral Advantage*, a classic study of morally motivated business leaders. The moral sentiments that constrain economic life also promote it. By creating the trust on which the market economy depends, these sentiments place the one who possesses them in the securest position to succeed in business.

The cost/benefit model of the human being is wrong in another and deeper respect. We are moral beings, in all the ways that Adam Smith describes. But we are also spiritual beings. We seek out the transcendental source of our values. We join with others in acts of worship and prayer. Through spiritual discipline, habit and exercise, we absorb the legacy of spiritual knowledge that is contained in a religious tradition. It is hard to put this knowledge into words—or into other words than are provided by worship and prayer. But for all that, it is real knowledge, which guides us in our daily lives and points us along the path to success.

This is a lesson that people are beginning to learn, as can be seen by typing the words "spirit work" into any search engine; Google produces a hundred million entries. More and more businesses are recognizing that their success depends upon providing some kind of spiritual satisfaction, and not just material satisfaction, to their workforce. The International Center for Spirit at Work is dedicated to encouraging businesses to take the spiritual life of their employees seriously. Leading businesses around the world—SREI International, for instance, and the Times of India—have begun to implement policies and programs designed to foster spiritual values in the workplace. One study, *A Spiritual Audit of Corporate America*, found that executives were eager to discover models for practicing spirituality in the workplace. But because such models are few and far between, and impossible to detach from the faith of the person who makes use of them, executives were often reluctant to take action, for fear of trampling on sensitivities and giving offense. The highly influential book *Megatrends*, which predicted the arrival of the information economy, and the recent sequel *Megatrends 2010*, predicting an "economy of consciousness," argue that the rise of spirituality in the workplace is "a trend that is about to become a megatrend." Others see the rise of the "spirit at work" movement as part of a nationwide attempt to compensate for the fragility of the old institutions, notably family and school, through which spiritual values were transmitted. Even Harvard Business School has recently made a point of introducing spiritual values into some of its courses.

In those and other ways we see the corporate world turning in the direction that I discuss in this book. For all the talk about the "spirit" and "spiritual values," however, there has been little recognition of the fundamental spiritual fact, which is the fact of faith. All too often people use the term "spiritual" to denote the hunger for meaning that remains when all bodily appetites have been satisfied. The spiritual comes to signify a kind of functionless residue of human activity, a place of bewilderment to which we arrive when all our immediate goals are transcended and the question of meaning stares us in the face. True faith is the opposite of that: not a residue but a source, a fount of wisdom and inspiration that leads and generates action and provides the real purpose in all that we say and do.

Of course, there are many different faiths, and nobody favors preaching one or another of them in the workplace. Not only would that be a gross infringement on freedom of conscience—a value upon which our society depends for its openness and its remarkable ability to acknowledge difference and defuse potential conflicts—it would be as likely to alienate as to inspire the audience. Nevertheless, in referring to spiritual capital I do not mean merely the spiritual hunger that frequents the modern workplace, or the forms of meditation, counseling or assembly that a firm might provide in order to satisfy it. I mean faith and all that stems from it, as these bequests are *applied* in business, by the one who possesses or makes use of them. My argument here is that there really is such a thing as spiritual capital, which has an economic function and economic potential comparable to other forms of capital, and which is used in business in the way that social capital is used.

On the other hand, this is not a book of apologetics or narrow theology; it is about the sources of business success. In referring to spiritual capital I am acknowledging the great amplification of the human spirit that comes through faith. In worship and prayer we entrust ourselves to another and greater power, and we learn to live through trust. In referring our decisions to that higher power we become more confident in making them. And in adopting the discipline and humility that come from religion we make ourselves ready to account for our failings and to deal honestly with others.

A religious tradition is not an arbitrary or invented thing. It emerges over many generations from the spiritual needs of a community. And it enshrines the accumulated wisdom that people achieve through rehearsing sacred stories, pondering examples and learning to acknowledge their faults. This kind of wisdom cannot be contained in a formula. It is not taught in business classes. It exists in and through faith, and its most easily recognizable manifestation is in the virtues of the one who possesses it. Those who believe that you can be successful in business without faith are of course right: you can be successful in any sphere, provided you have luck and skill and trust in your own powers. But often you will be drawing on spiritual capital that has been built up by others and is stored in the virtues of a workforce or the customs of a market. And it is worth pointing out that businesspeople in America and elsewhere are very far from the picture of the pragmatic and self-seeking atheist that is the favored TV caricature of their stereotyped social role. In a study of American elites, sociologists discovered that, next to military officers and church professionals, more businesspeople attended church every week than any other elite: twice as many as congressional aides, four times as many as news-media professionals, nine times as many as elites of the TV and movie industries.

This correlation between professional business and religious faith ought not to surprise us. Only the discredited caricature of business—as a zero-sum game in which every person's profit is someone else's loss, and in which the ruthless pursuit of profit is the sole purpose of the game—persuades people to overlook what surely ought to be obvious: that in business you expose yourself to criticism, take risks, acquire heavy debts of responsibility and accountability, and are thrust into moral relation with others, in ways that demand a far more robust and serious morality than is needed to survive in some cushioned state bureaucracy or in a comfortable academic chair. Business is the real test of the moral life, and those who engage in it are putting themselves in a position where trust in God's goodness is the surest guarantee of success.

This is not the only reason why so many businesspeople are religiously devout, however. If we study the workings of spiritual capital, we will see that its principal manifestation lies in the virtues of individual people. Worship and prayer are not isolated parts of a human life; they are ways of disciplining the spirit so that it listens to and is guided by a higher power. And the immediate result is the shaping of the human character, which in turn transforms culture—national as well as corporate. Vices lose their attraction and virtues become easier as spiritual discipline exerts its hold over the human personality. Of course, atheists and agnostics can be virtuous people too. But they lack one easy and transparent route to virtue, which is the path of prayer.

That said, it is worth looking at the topic of virtue from a more secular and classical perspective, in order to convince the reader that there really is such a thing and that it really does have a function in the life of business. In subsequent chapters I will explore the connection between virtue and the religious way of life as manifest in business.

 *2. Virtue*

> I tell you that virtue is not given by money, but that
> from virtue comes money, and every other good,
> public as well as private.
>
> *Socrates*

IT IS CHARACTERISTIC OF THE AGE in which we live to see the moral life as a matter of following rules or dictated principles. Whether discoverable by reason or laid down by God, these rules are what we must teach our children and what we ourselves must follow. This emphasis on rule-guided conduct is common to those, like Kant, who put duty at the heart of moral thinking, and equally to those, like Bentham and the utilitarians, who shift our attention from the dutiful motive to the useful effect.

Ancient writers seldom referred to rules or principles. For them the moral life was not a matter of what you *do* but of what you *are*. The fundamental notion was not duty but virtue (Latin *virtus*, Greek *areté*), and the task of the moralist was to describe the virtues that we should emulate and teach to our children. This is how Socrates, Plato and—pre-eminently—Aristotle conceived the moral life. The Romans followed the same path, and it is interesting to note that the words of Cicero and Quintilian closely correspond to thoughts uttered some centuries earlier in China by the great sage Confucius. Like Confucius, the Greeks and Romans attempted to find a basis for moral conduct in human nature. And like Confucius, they believed that the core idea is virtue.

Alasdair MacIntyre has argued, in his classic *After Virtue*, that the "liberal individualism" of the Enlightenment tried to replace the old ethic of virtue with an ethic of freely chosen yet objectively binding rules. But because the search for such rules will always be frustrated, this attempt has led to the relativism and rootlessness that we perceive around us today.

MacIntyre wishes to redirect our moral thinking towards the idea of virtue, and this I wholly applaud. But where is virtue to be found in the modern world, and which institutions promote it? MacIntyre gives no answer. But there is an answer to be found, I suggest, in business. The "little platoons" that, according to Burke, shape the moral sense and character of the individual, and that Tocqueville saw as the moral backbone of the young American democracy, find their most vivid and confident manifestation in the world of business. And businesses led by faith create the moral space required by virtue. By respecting the spirit, we enable it to grow as it should.

Aristotle saw virtue as constitutive of happiness. The benefits conferred by the virtues were first and foremost benefits to the individual who possessed them, rather than the community of which he was a part. Aristotle went further and actually defined happiness in terms of virtue: happiness (*eudaimonia*) is "an activity of the soul in accordance with virtue." This definition is as valid today as when Aristotle first presented it as a cornerstone of his ethical theory, though it goes quite against the teachings of the modern "happiness experts," whose attempts to measure happiness actually reduce it to a succession of momentary pleasures. Happiness, Aristotle made clear, is not composed of fleeting sensations available equally to selfless and selfish people. It involves a settled contentment with one's lot, with oneself and with others. It is not an experience but a condition, in which we flourish according to our nature, as a tree flourishes in healthy soil, or a fish in pure water.

We can achieve this condition, Aristotle argued, only through the virtues. We teach our children to be courageous, wise, just and temperate because we know that this will make them respected by their fellows, secure in their decisions, and able to take full responsibility for their lives. That is the way to happiness. It is also the way in which the individual serves the community: the happiness of the individual and the prosperity of the community are both achieved through virtue.

Success in business is similar. Success may spring from a lucky accident. But lucky accidents cannot be planned. We prepare for success by acquiring virtues—dispositions that help us to take risks, to make decisions, to take responsibility for our actions, and to accept wise advice. These virtues are the most important part of our human capital. We do not invent them for ourselves. Instead, they grow organically over time, through history, tradition and experience, and they are crystallized in the examples set by worthy action. The knowledge gained from tradition and example is, like virtue, out of favor. Abstract theories and bodies of "universal" rules are held out as the hallmarks of real knowledge, while tradition and example are regarded as incomplete and parochial, hence not knowledge. Yet the virtues form part of our collective inheritance. Through faith, tradition and religious discipline we adopt them into ourselves. That is why we need to speak of spiritual capital.

Philosophers and moralists have tended to agree with Aristotle's list of the cardinal virtues—temperance, courage, justice and practical wisdom (*phronesis*). By calling these virtues cardinal (from Latin *cardo*, a hinge), we emphasize that all else turns on them: that without them no other virtues can be reliably acquired or exercised. But what is meant by calling them virtues? When I say that it is a virtue in a horse that it is steady in traffic, or a virtue in a chair that it is comfortable to sit in, I am relating the horse or the chair to the world of human interests. Being steady in traffic is an equine feature in which we, as riders, have an interest. From our point of view, the steadier, the better. When I speak of the virtues of a human being, however, I mean something more far-reaching. I do not mean that one is useful

to others. I mean that one has habits that contribute to human fulfillment, and to one's own fulfillment first of all. We all have an interest
in each other's character; but we also have a commanding interest in
our own character and what we do with it. That is why we distinguish
virtues from vices, recognizing that our most intimate self-conception will be affected by our habits, and that good habits bring not just
success in our endeavors, but inner tranquility and peace of mind.

Aristotle also was of this opinion. The context in which he developed his argument—the context of the Greek city-state, existing in
fierce commercial and military competition with its neighbors—was
very far from the context in which a modern corporation operates.
Nevertheless, his argument was aimed at what is permanent in human
nature, with a view to identifying the qualities that people need in all
the circumstances of life if they are to achieve the fulfillment that is
within their capacity. He saw virtues as dispositions, which we learn
by imitation and habit, but which are something more than knee-jerk
reactions. The virtuous person does not merely acquire new and more
disciplined behavior; he acquires new and more fulfilling *motives*. To
be genuinely courageous, it is not sufficient to imitate the actions of a
courageous person; in advance of the circumstances it is impossible
to know what those actions will be. To be courageous is to be moved
as the courageous person is moved. It is to desire what is honorable
and good, despite the cost in terms of personal discomfort and danger. The point about virtue is that it is reliable; and people become
reliable when they are motivated in the right way. In a time of danger we look to the courageous person because we know that he will
put the common good above his own personal safety, and therefore,
through his leadership and example, create the best chance that the
present danger will be overcome.

The Greeks saw virtue as a unity. Each of the four cardinal virtues
depends upon and amplifies the others. A courageous person must

be temperate if he is not to overstep the mark. Intemperate courage is not courage but rashness, and temperance in turn needs courage if it is to show its proper worth—the courage to face up to temptation and to the pressure of one's peers and still say no. But one of the great difficulties that the Greek philosophers faced was that of integrating justice into their moral scheme. We can justify courage, temperance and wisdom as benefits to the person who possesses them—traits of character that bring success, and which make it maximally probable that the person who possesses them will overcome the difficulties that beset us in the trials of life. But justice is a much more "other-regarding" virtue, and the question "why be just?" troubled the Greek philosophers as it has troubled every thinking person since. It is the question that launches the argument of Plato's *Republic*. And it is the question addressed by the Greek poets and tragedians in their most memorable bequests to us. It is also a question that bears directly on the conduct of business, and which we will approach from many angles in the chapters that follow.

Aristotle defined the virtue of justice as the disposition to give each person his due; and this is the definition taken up centuries later by Ulpian in his digest of Roman law. All rational beings need justice, Aristotle argued, since all need the cooperation of their fellows and the trust on which it depends. Moreover, without justice there is no friendship, since the friend is the one who both gives what is due and receives it. The most interesting feature of Aristotle's discussion of justice is his recognition that it is a quality of the individual and of the individual action. Justice is something that we do, and which we are blamed for not doing. It has its root and motive in the virtue of justice—the virtue displayed by the person who sees others as his equals and who responds instinctively to their rightful demands.

Aristotle's notion of justice is also grounded in a disposition that is entirely internal to the person. That is, for Aristotle, justice begins as a personal virtue, even though it ultimately has a social application as well. The internal, personal dimension of justice is the ability or habit of governing conflicting internal desires and motives in a "just" or fair manner. By learning to preside over the inner conflicts of personality and desire, one becomes just, and so develops abilities to lead in society as well. In other words, self-government in the classical view is the foundation for leadership in society.

That ancient conception of justice has been overlaid in modern times by a rival idea, which sees justice as a feature of "society," not of individual actions. The concept of "social or public justice" gained a hold during the nineteenth century under the influence of Christian social thought. It has a large part to play in the Calvinist theories of Abraham Kuyper, the theologian who was briefly prime minister of the Netherlands at the turn of the twentieth century. And there is a powerful tradition within Catholic theology that also sees "social justice" as a primary obligation of the Church. The modern opponents of capitalism make much of the "social injustices" that it supposedly creates and sustains; and they often frame their demands in terms of an ideal of "social justice"—as in the celebrated work of John Rawls (*A Theory of Justice*).

According to the Christian tradition, "social or public justice" means a proper regulation of society, so that people can deal justly with each other in the *several* communities to which they belong. Social justice requires that we maintain the separate spheres of social interaction, so that each can be guided by its own spontaneous form of order—the order of the family, the club, the firm, the regiment, the school. This is what Kuyper originally understood by social justice: not the control of society by the state, but the retreat of the state from the self-governing spheres where it is not needed. A similar doctrine has been upheld by the Catholic Church under the name of "subsidiarity," meaning the freedom of social institutions to govern themselves. The

Catholic doctrine was adopted by capitalism in order to show how a capitalist economy can be reconciled with social justice, by supporting the institutions of civil society through which people help each other and relieve the stresses of competition.

In the modern context, however, "social justice" has too often become a term of anticapitalist rhetoric, and it is typically held to require redistribution of goods by the state. In other words, it has come to mean the confiscation of property by bureaucrats who have no personal responsibility either in the matter of acquiring it or in the matter of giving it away. This use of the concept involves severing the idea of justice from that of individual accountability. And it condones the compulsory seizure of assets irrespective of whether they were justly or unjustly acquired. It is precisely this conception of social justice that authorized the great crimes committed in our day in the name of socialism and communism. And it is "social justice" under-stood in the socialist way that has crippled the capitalist economies of Europe, to the great disadvantage of everyone, including those whom "social justice" is supposed to benefit.

By seeing justice as a virtue of individuals, however, we help to reintegrate the demand for justice into a healthy and creative econ-omy. Justice regulates and upholds contracts; it encourages respect in the workplace and accountability both to customers and to share-holders. It distinguishes the phony demands of interlopers from the rightful demands of those to whom something is owed. And it fur-thers the long-term relationships of trust on which a successful busi-ness and the larger community both depend. By emphasizing the classical virtue as the core of justice, we once again put justice within our reach and enable it to exert its benign influence over our actions. This does not mean that we can ignore the social conditions that sur-round us: evidently, where there is large-scale discrimination against minorities or blatant disregard of civil rights, justice demands that we take a stand on behalf of those who are being thus mistreated. But the important point is contained in that last word: for there to be injustice, there must be mistreatment. Someone must be *in the wrong*, and justice demands that the wrong be righted.

Our Judeo-Christian tradition has retained the core of Aristotle's idea of virtue and added virtues of its own. It has also distanced itself from some of the dispositions that Aristotle wished to include in his list of admirable qualities, and which reflect the vanished social context of the Greek city-state. St. Thomas Aquinas devotes many pages to the discussion of virtue in the *Summa theologiae*, taking Aristotle and Augustine as his guides. His most important emendation to the Aristotelian position lies in the emphasis he accords to charity as the highest of the virtues. According to Aquinas, charity is the virtue without which no other virtue is manifest in its perfected form. In this, Aquinas is following St. Paul's famous evocation of charity in I Corinthians 13. Charity (Latin *caritas*) is a translation of the Greek *agape*, the New Testament name for the love that we can offer to everyone, the "love to which we are commanded," as Kant put it. The ability to offer this love is a virtue, requiring the highest moral discipline; and the acquisition of this virtue is the aim and achievement of the Christian faith.

Aquinas agrees with the ancient theory of the unity of the cardinal virtues; he goes further, however, insisting that all virtues form a unity in their perfect forms. Virtues exist in three forms: the cardinal virtues, which are the *sine qua non* without which there can be no virtue; the virtues devoted to human well-being, which depend upon prudence; and perfect virtues, or the virtues in their perfected form. No perfect virtue can be had without charity, and if charity is had, then all of them are had. (*Disputed Questions*, 119.) What Aquinas means by this is that informing every virtue in its perfect form is the charitable motive—the motive that looks with love on the individual human being, and which places the interests of others at the heart of all that it intends. Aquinas quotes Augustine with approval:

> The prudence of misers by which they think up all sorts of ways to make a little money is not true virtue, nor their justice when fear of heavy losses for themselves makes them despise the rights of others, nor again their temperance which makes them restrain their lust because it costs too much to indulge, nor their courage which drives them, as Horace says, to cross oceans, scale rocks and go through flames to avoid poverty. (*Contra Julianum* IV, 3, quoted *Summa theologiae*, 2a2ae, 23, 7.)

Like Aristotle, in his discussion of justice, Aquinas is claiming that the good conferred on the individual by his own virtues is conferred on him because those virtues put him into creative and reciprocal relation with others. This is what St. Paul meant in his letter to the Corinthians. Christ enjoined us to charity because this is the way in which we imbue ourselves and others with the love of God, and so bring our own nature to perfection.

Aquinas distinguishes St. Paul's three leading virtues—faith, hope and charity—as the "theological virtues," the virtues that govern our relation with God, emphasizing however that the human virtues discussed by Aristotle are perfected only when joined to the theological virtues. Although Aristotle believed that the highest good for mankind resides in the knowledge and contemplation of God, the emphasis on faith as an active engagement with the world, on hope as a vision of eternity and on charity as a constant goodwill towards others connotes a specifically Christian approach to life in this world. Later Christian writers—and in particular reformers such as Luther and Calvin and the Protestant divines—emphasized other aspects of virtue, while retaining the outline bequeathed by St. Thomas. My readers will have their own sense of which qualities are most important in preparing a person for the free exercise of responsible choice. The list that I give reflects a particular tradition of religious thought, as well as a particular set of telling examples. In all cases, however, I will try to show the way in which virtue is not merely beneficial to business, but also amplified by the spiritual aspect of human life.

The Virtues of Business

FAITH. First among the virtues that belong to spiritual capital is this, the defining feature. The word comes from the Latin *fides*, meaning trust. In the practical sphere, faith implies an allegiance to duty or faithfulness to one's promises. In the spiritual sphere, it implies both sincerity of intentions and a belief in and loyalty to God. Religious faith involves trust in the existence and benevolence of something for which there is no proof. It is the virtue that brings complete trust in the righteousness of creation, and thereby fills life with purpose.

In the next chapter I shall explore the connection between faith, hope and charity, how they function together in creating a flourishing business, and why we should still see these virtues as embodying our bequest of spiritual capital and the ideal preparation for success in this life as well as hope for the next.

The writer of Hebrews defined faith as "the substance of things hoped for, the evidence of things not seen." As this definition states, faith is a dynamic link between the world as it actually exists and the realm of what is yet unseen but hoped for. Somehow, faith makes hope tangible and makes the invisible evident. Faith changes things. Thus, faith is clearly integral to the character and action of the entrepreneur who converts invisible hope into tangible substance. Transcendent actions that transform the world are acts of faith.

HONESTY. The business virtue *par excellence*, honesty is a quality without which markets cannot long survive. It reflects an upright character, a devotion to the truth, and a refusal to lie, steal or deceive. It is the greatest benefit that a businessperson can confer on those he deals with, and also the greatest benefit that he can confer on himself, since it is the quality that enables others to trust him. "Honesty is the best policy": so says the proverb. But it is not because honesty is the best policy that we should be honest. Rather, it is because we are honest that our endeavors are marked by success. Honesty is an integral part of justice as the Greeks conceived it, and the concepts of truth and justice are often contained in a single word—"right" in English, *Recht* in German, *haqq* in Arabic, and so on.

GRATITUDE. From the same Latin root as grace, gracefulness and graciousness, gratitude is the disposition to acknowledge gifts. It is a sign of humility and maturity, a powerful source of joy, healing, contentment and lasting relationships. Its role in business has been insufficiently appreciated. Arguably, however, it is the person who gives thanks for what he receives who best knows how to value it, and also how to attain it. One of the most remarkable achievements of European socialism has been to create a society from which gratitude has all but disappeared. When all benefits are promised by the state, nobody need feel grateful for them, nor does anybody feel the impulse to return the gift. Virtually nobody who benefits from college in Europe gives back to his *alma mater,* and all institutions, from schools to hospitals, look to the state for their support. It is one of the strengths of a capitalist economy that it reminds people at every point of the great gifts they receive from others and from the free exercise of human choice. Hence a capitalist economy such as we enjoy here in America is one in which people are constantly giving back to their schools, universities, local communities, churches and hospitals some part of what they have been fortunate enough to earn.

PERSEVERANCE. This virtue is one that religion strengthens in ways that are most needful in the world of commerce. God responds to the persistent prayers of his children (Matthew 7:7), and we are encouraged to keep asking, keep seeking, keep knocking. This discipline is hard, but without it we are prone to despair, dereliction or vacillation, and thereby can easily lose our way.

COMPASSION. From Latin *compati*, to sympathize or "suffer with," this virtue is placed at the heart of human life by the great religions, and spreads its gift both on the one who suffers and on the one who "suffers with." Many people, both the opponents of capitalism and certain of its defenders, have seen compassion as alien to the business agenda. Described by Nietzsche as the morality of the slave, compassion—which is the core of morality for Christian, Muslim, Hindu, Buddhist and Jew—was rejected also by Ayn Rand in her influential defense of capitalism as the expression of human freedom and power, with the telling title *The Virtue of Selfishness*. For Rand and her followers, the essence of the free economy is individualism and self-assertion. Others may benefit from this, but only if the entrepreneur is not distracted by compassion from his primary and rightful goal, which is his own success.

Many people see capitalism in Darwinian terms, as a constant struggle for scarce resources, in which only the fittest survive. But once we see that the capitalist economy is not an arena of conflict over pre-existing resources, but a cooperative attempt to bring those resources into being—once we see, in other words, that capitalism is about the mutual creation of wealth rather than the antagonistic pillaging of it—we will recognize the place of compassion in business. Compassion enables us to pursue our goals without conflict, by arousing the sympathy and goodwill of others. It makes us flexible in the face of opposition and gives us insight into the feelings and desires of those with whom we have to deal. The kind of self-assertion extolled by Rand is really a brittleness of character, an unyielding self-centeredness that is soon fractured by the conflicts it engenders.

FORGIVENESS. From the old English *forgifan*, forgiveness means giving up resentments or claims to requital against someone who has offended you. Fundamental to the Christian vision, forgiveness must be understood as a process—not a failure to perceive the offense, but an acknowledgment of it and a going out to meet the offender, so as to renew the relationship that has been damaged. Forgiveness cleanses the spirit from the poison of anger and hate, and it is as important in the marketplace as it is in private life. Later I shall illustrate the point with examples; but it is worth emphasizing at this juncture that forgiveness is one of the hardest virtues to acquire, and is often almost impossible to acquire without prayer. Those who have been through concentration camps, who have been targeted by persecution, who have been wrongly exposed to injury and contempt by those who have power over them, have only one weapon against the accumulated weight of disasters, and that is forgiveness. Yet all such people testify to the immense spiritual labor that forgiveness, in these circumstances, requires.

PATIENCE. From the Latin *pati*, to suffer. To bear pains and trials calmly and without complaint is difficult. But this disposition is needful for all those who wish to triumph over adversity and to persist in their aims. Patience focuses our efforts on what we can change, while accepting what we cannot change. It is the virtue of the martyr, and also of the dogged commander, who never loses sight of the goal. Patience is enjoined upon us by faith. Jews and Christians alike treasure the book of Job, which shows patience as the sublime refuge that faith alone can guarantee. But patience rests on other virtues. A verse of the Koran reminds us "to seek help with patience and prayer, and this is indeed hard, except for the humble in spirit" (2, v. 46). Hence the need for humility.

HUMILITY. From the Latin *humilis*, meaning low in status, humility is the first virtue of the spiritual life. Every virtue not tempered by humility will turn to conceit and narcissism. When God grants a talent, we learn to ask for humility so as properly to enjoy it and to make it useful to others. The role of humility in business is difficult to describe. But it has been attested by many business leaders, and in my examples I will try to show its spiritual source. Humility is also tied through the French source of the word to the mutual relation between a rider and horse, close to the concept of dressage or mastery through cooperation.

COURAGE. From Latin *cor*, meaning heart, courage is the disposition to pursue our projects, despite every difficulty and danger. Only if we believe that we are right to do as we do can we face the dangers that beset us in doing it. Hence courage involves a strong power of moral judgment, a recognition that there is a real distinction between right and wrong. Aristotle recognized this; he described the motive of courage as that which is good or honorable (*to kalon*) and regarded all acts of boldness done from some other motive as mere rashness or bravado.

RESPECT. From Latin *respectus*, a looking back, respect means acknowledging others as your moral and spiritual equals, recognizing their right to be treated with dignity, and making no exceptions in your own favor. Advocates of "social justice" often criticize the world of business as an offense against justice, generating as it does such unequal distributions of wealth. How is the capitalist economy compatible, people ask, with the "respect for persons" that demands equal treatment for all? The answer, in a nutshell, is that equal treatment produces unequal outcomes, while the attempt to secure an equal outcome will always require unequal treatment of individuals. We should see respect as one form of the Aristotelian virtue of justice—the disposition to accord others their due, and therefore to acknowledge that rights, deserts and entitlements depend upon what the individual himself has done. Respect means, thus, to pay heed or pay attention, and to give what is appropriate and owed to each, to equals equally, and to unequals unequally. It is unfair to give the same to everyone without *respect* to what they do.

GENEROSITY. From the Latin *generare*, to beget or produce, generosity is the disposition to give what is honestly asked for, to support others through their times of hardship, and to be open-handed in disposing of one's goods. *Generosus* means noble as well as magnanimous, and the Romans saw this virtue as one that befits a higher social status, since it reconciles those who enjoy that status to those who do not. In our less class-ridden society we see generosity as the natural way to show love and friendship, knowing that without it we become isolated from our fellows.

DISCIPLINE. From the same Latin root as "disciple," discipline implies the ability to learn from example, to follow a rule or order of life and to set temptation aside. This is the virtue that begins in obedience and flowers in self-control. It involves restraint, an ability to accept privations and to resist temptation. But it is not incompatible with magnanimity. It requires discipline of the heart and the mind to obey John Wesley's Rule: Do all the good you can, by all the means you can, in all the ways you can, in all the places you can, at all the times you can, to all the people you can, as long as ever you can. Or Aristotle's rule for virtue: do the right thing for the right reason at the right time to the right degree in the right manner. To follow such a rule requires a settled temperament, an ability to ignore distractions, and an inner resolve.

CHASTITY. This virtue has gotten a bad name in contemporary culture. A vast industry has been devoted to driving chastity out of the way in which human relations are conceived, and this industry has had its effect on business, just as it has undermined much of public life. For all the preaching in favor of "sexual liberation," it remains as true today as it has ever been that people admire chastity and regard breaches of sexual decorum with distaste. We know from the example of a recent president that unchaste behavior, when discovered, may lead to personal trauma and public disgrace. And unchaste behavior at work can lead to a collapse in trust, as employees are exposed to sexual predation, and jealousies and rivalries prevail over equable relations.

The Greeks saw chastity as a part of temperance—but were none too clear as to what it required in men. We now make no distinction between men and women, and require the same restraint, while allowing the same permission, to both. Hence it is all the more important, in business as in other fields, to maintain the kind of boundaries that enable people to enjoy just and charitable relations that are protected from sexual invasion. It is undeniable that faith has had an important function in this respect, and chastity is invariably one of the first casualties of the loss of faith.

THRIFT. This virtue too has come in for some disparaging commentary in recent discussions, the *cheapskate* being routinely dismissed in something like the terms with which Dickens dismissed Ebeneezer Scrooge. Yet for our ancestors, thrift stood shoulder to shoulder with honesty in the code of good commerce, and was indeed regarded as a fundamental part of virtue in every sphere. Thus Webster, in 1828, defined thrift in laudatory terms:

> Economical in the use or appropriation of money, goods or provisions of any kind; saving unnecessary expense, either of money or any thing else which is to be used or consumed; sparing; not profuse, prodigal or lavish. We ought to be frugal not only in the expenditure of money and of goods, but in the employment of time. Prudent economy; good husbandry or housewifery; a sparing use or appropriation of money or commodities; a judicious use of any thing to be expended or employed; that careful

management which expends nothing unnecessarily, and applies
what is used to a profitable purpose; nothing is wasted. It is not
equivalent to parsimony, the latter being an excess to a fault.
Thrift is always a virtue.

If there is any truth in Weber's thesis that the Calvinist spirit was
fundamental to the birth of capitalism, it lies in the centrality of the
virtue of thrift in the Calvinist worldview. In this, as in most things,
Calvin was emphasizing longstanding insights of the biblical tradition. The notion of the *daily bread* that sustains us and the labor that
is involved in providing it and which is built into the very structure
of creation is highlighted continually by Calvin. "Yet our Lord com-
menced with bread and the supports of an earthly life, that from
such a beginning he might carry us higher." (John Calvin, *Commentary* on Matthew 6:31–43.) Calvin is teaching his followers to endure
patiently and in a spirit of humility and not to be "intoxicated by a
false confidence in earthly abundance." For Calvin, "our bread" is a
metaphor for *all* goods and belongings. But these are not literally *our*
bread. Calvin states:

> It is so called, not because it belongs to us by right, but because the
> fatherly kindness of God has set it apart for our use. It becomes
> ours, because our heavenly Father freely bestows it on us for the
> supplies of our necessities. The fields must no doubt be culti-
> vated, labor must be bestowed on gathering the fruits of the earth,
> and every man must submit to the toil of his calling, in order to
> procure food. But all this does not hinder us from being fed by the
> undeserved kindness of God, without which men might waste
> their strength to no purpose. We are thus taught, that what we
> seem to have acquired by our own industry is His *gift.*

Caring for God's endowment in a thrifty fashion is here a form of biblical obedience. Some would contrast this with the Baconian notion

that the world is ours to exploit. Calvin taught that the commandments in the first chapters of Genesis would instruct us to "build and to keep," which suggests a proper balance, not a mandate to pillage. This balance is part of the role of thrift, which is to help us distinguish between what we want and what we need. It is also a balance between oneself and the world. There is a deep connection between thrift and gratitude, and both are linked to a proper consideration for others and their needs.

Hence, while Calvin extolled thrift as a part of stewardship, he did so in the context of a community in which charity towards the neighbor was held to be the binding principle. Calvin believed that, just as the rich had a responsibility to the poor, so too the poor had a mission to the rich. The poor were the receivers of God, the vicars of Christ, the solicitors of God who offer the rich an opportunity to free themselves from monetary slavery and to be saved from greed.

Weber was thus only half right in connecting the rise of capitalism to the Calvinist emphasis on thrift, for he missed the other and major point. For Calvin, as for others in the Judaeo-Christian tradition, thrift is essential to a community founded in generosity. Calvin did not legislate generosity in the manner of the Islamic *zakat*—the obligation to give a proportion of one's goods to charity; rather, he called his followers to take the *rule of love* as their guide. The life of thrift is also a life of gratitude. The citizens of Calvin's Geneva were to be grateful for all that they had been given, not for themselves but as stewards until, in Calvin's words, "such time as they came to behold the face of Him whose love had never let them go."

Thrift, seen in this way, is intimately connected with the virtuous forms of giving. The point has been made eloquently for our times in *Thrift and Generosity: The Joy of Giving*; but it goes back all the way to Aristotle, who included prudence and liberality among the virtues and suggested that in the end they mutually require each other.

Spiritual Entrepreneurship

The list of virtues can be extended, though each addition goes over ground already covered. The more we consider in detail what the virtues involve, the more we recognize that they are interconnected in just the way that Aristotle and Aquinas believed. Reciting a list of the virtues recalls the Sufi ritual of enunciating the names of God: one is moving from one aspect to another of a single essence. The virtues that I have listed contribute to success in every realm of human endeavor, and not just in business. They are universally applicable forms of human excellence, which it is rational for each of us to pursue.

There are also virtues that are more specifically connected to the business sphere. Many have identified what are called the three cardinal virtues of business: creativity, building community and practical realism. These are not qualities that we demand or can demand of everyone, but certainly they are qualities that contribute to business success and also vindicate the place of business in society. In what follows, we will see both individual virtues and those specifically "business virtues" in the circumstances that put them to the test. In giving examples from the modern economy I will be illustrating the way in which God-fearing, God-loving people make choices shaped by personal faith and religious tradition. And these choices guide them towards success.

We should not be surprised by this success. The laws of economic life are subject to the eternal laws enshrined in our spiritual capital. Those who believe in God's love do not doubt that He intended his creatures to enjoy the fruits of their activity, and in doing so to benefit all those with whom they openly and honestly deal. The workings of the market are shaped by Providence, and those whose faith enables them to perceive and act on this momentous fact are already turned towards success. Spiritual entrepreneurship is therefore the unsung route to growth in the modern economy.

We live in times of great challenge. Old economies are fragmenting under the impact of global trade; new technologies are rapidly displacing the old, and the information revolution is now making itself felt around the world. Old styles of business are giving way to the new "stakeholder" model—a model that I shall subject to examination in the final chapter—and in every sphere, choices are expanding and prohibitions withering under the impact of the Internet. Some react to these changes with glum despair, believing that our old ways of doing things are under siege and that we will soon be swamped by chaos or by our competitors. On the contrary, we live in a world of opportunities, and our need is for the key that will unlock them and open the avenues to yet greater economic success. This key is spiritual entrepreneurship, which directs the vast inheritance of spiritual capital that we enjoy towards the new challenges of the global economy.

3. Faith, Hope and Charity

To thee only God granted a heart ever new, To all
always open, To all always true.

Matthew Arnold

THE FIRST AND MOST IMPORTANT COMPONENT in spiritual entrepreneurship is faith. There is a temptation to think of faith merely as a belief—the belief that God exists and that he will reward the good and punish the bad. People of faith know how misleading such ideas are. Faith is not just belief but knowledge—knowledge of a person and that presence in your life. Faith means enjoying a personal relation with the Creator and learning to put your trust in him. It is through faith that people can most easily take those risks from which enterprises begin, and it is faith that enables people to confront defeats and setbacks and to win through to ultimate success.

In a study that forms the basis for a series of books on the role of moral values in business, it was found that over 90 percent of the businesspeople interviewed expressed a devout spiritual or religious faith. This doesn't mean that successful business leaders are constantly preaching and proselytizing in the workplace; on the contrary, they normally believe in freedom of conscience and the need to be private about one's deepest beliefs. It means, rather, that the vast majority of business leaders in the study sought God's guidance and were fortified and comforted by bringing their problems and choices to him.

Nor is it unusual, particularly in the American context, to find personal faith explicitly incorporated in the aims of a business. Consider Dacor, the kitchen appliance company founded in 1965 by Stan Joseph and now led by Stan's son, Mike. Dacor's mission statement is "to honor God in all we do: by respecting others; by doing good work; by helping others; by forgiving others; by giving thanks; and by celebrating our lives." This statement brings into focus some of the virtues that I described in the last chapter and shows their importance in a life based in faith. No more than any other CEO does Mike Joseph preach in the workplace or demand of his workforce any particular set of religious beliefs. His firm is run on the spiritual capital provided by its leaders, and this generates the atmosphere of mutual respect and goodwill that prevails in the workplace, encouraging employees to feel wanted not as tools but as people, and thereby releasing their creative potential. The fact that Dacor is a fast-growing and highly innovative business and a leader in its field may reasonably be attributed to the faith that is embodied in its mission statement.

Of course, faith can play its part in founding and expanding a business, even when it is not explicitly mentioned in such a statement or put on public display. Interesting in this respect is the story of Domino's Pizza, which began life in 1960 when an orphan boy, Tom Monaghan, with $500 of savings, decided to join with his brother Nick in opening a pizza delivery store in Ypsilanti, Michigan, which they called DomiNick's. A year later, Monaghan traded his Volkswagen Beetle for his brother's share in the store, renamed the business Domino's, and set out to open three stores. Monaghan's guiding principles were to meet the highest standards in his product, and at the same time to be a positive member of the communities where his stores were situated. He saw his venture as an act of service to others, and his Catholic faith supported this view. As the reputation of his business grew, he decided to expand through franchises—a little-known practice at the time, and one that raised the question of trust in its acutest form. His solution was to demand that his franchisees be committed to the community, designing their stores sympathetically, employing local people, showing respect for the environment and supporting local charitable causes. His faith in God brought with it a trust of others, and by trusting he made himself trusted. Soon the competition for Domino's Pizza franchises began to gather momentum, and Domino's became a household name. When Tom sold the company in 1998, he made a billion dollars.

The story doesn't end there. In gratitude for what he had been given through his faith, Tom Monaghan decided to make a gift in turn. He gave away most of his profit to charity, and in particular to the founding of institutions that would help consolidate the faith that had inspired him. It is thanks to Tom Monaghan that Ave Maria University in Florida now exists: a new campus with innovative faculty, dedicated to upholding the Christian contribution to the American cultural heritage and to propagating objective knowledge in the social sciences.

St. Paul connected faith with hope and charity as the three virtues on which a Christian life is founded. In Tom Monaghan's case we see clearly the route that begins in faith, breeds hope as its byproduct, and ends not in material success only, but in the thing that justifies success and makes it all worthwhile, namely charity towards one's neighbor and the desire to return to the community the good that one has derived from it.

Nor are the spiritual virtues a monopoly of the Christian faith. Instructive is the story of one of Domino's franchisees, Rumi Verjee, an Ismaili Muslim who came to England as a refugee from East Africa when Asians in the region began to suffer persecution in the wake of independence. Verjee had won a place at Cambridge, and after his studies he worked in lowly positions in the City of London, dreaming always of bettering himself and of rescuing his family's fortunes. He stayed close to his community while moving easily in English society, which he had been brought up to respect. And he treasured in his heart a meeting he had once had with Mother Teresa during a visit to his family in India. He had been impressed, as he put it, by her simplicity and naivety: her determination always to see good in others and to live life without resentment. This became Rumi Verjee's ideal, and he associated it both with Mother Teresa's faith and with his own faith in a God of compassion. In everything thereafter he felt himself guided by a higher power, to whom he prayed and in whom he trusted. Thanks to his faith, Verjee never lost the hope that he would be able to reverse the disasters that had befallen him and his family.

A natural businessman, Verjee studied the opportunities as they arose. Reading that Domino's Pizza wished to sell the British and Irish franchise, Verjee knew that he must acquire it. His determination to see good in others and to live without resentment, as Mother Teresa taught, meant that he was surrounded by a network of well-wishers. Hence he obtained promises of loans, and he wrote to Tom Monaghan proposing a meeting and expressing interest in the British and Irish franchise for Domino's. He received a reply from Tom Monaghan's office that no such request could be considered unless it came from a party with whom Domino's had had business dealings. Verjee persevered, with equal lack of success. Letter after letter led to nothing, and all attempts to reach Tom Monaghan through an intermediary failed. But Rumi never lost hope, sensing that a hand was guiding him and that he must trust that hand and give himself to it. He therefore flew across the Atlantic to attend the annual general meeting of Domino's shareholders, at which Tom Monaghan was to give a public speech. At the end of the speech, Verjee fought his way through the crowd to where his target was surrounded by the microphones and cameras of the press. The message he was able at last to convey was that Tom must agree to see him. And Tom directed Rumi to his personal assistant, who duly arranged the appointment.

Recognizing in Rumi the faith and trust by which he himself had been guided, Tom willingly granted the franchise, and from that moment Rumi never looked back. By the time he sold the British and Irish franchises, the profits were sufficient to enable Rumi Verjee to become one of the leading entrepreneurs in his community and a source of cohesion to all around him.

Verjee recognizes the connection between faith and charity. As he explains it:

> Although you can get on by being ruthless, by thinking of nothing but your own profit, and by rejoicing in others' loss, this is not the way to true success. Compassion is as important in a business-man as in any other human being. It is important not only for others' sake but also for your own. However successful you are, you are also a vulnerable human being, who will always need help and affection, and who stands to lose everything by being arro-gant. You can receive help only if you give it; and the same is true of love and affection. Like all Muslims, we Ismailis are taught to give to charity as a religious duty. But I mean something more than that obligatory giving. I mean that we should recognize that success brings duties as well as pleasures. As we rise to the top we should spare a thought for those at the bottom; and the pleasure of giving is surely one of the greatest rewards of success.

Virtues are seen at their most admirable in adversity, when they seal the fate of the one who has them. We know this from the virtue of courage. It is certain that the courageous person is more likely to succeed in life, since he will take the risks on which success depends. But it is also certain that in real adversity he is more at risk than the coward. Like the Spartans at Thermopylae, the courageous person will stand firm in the line of duty until cut down. This doesn't show courage to be irrational. On the contrary, it shows that the virtue we need to conduct ordinary life successfully may, in extraordinary cir-cumstances, expose us to danger. But the same virtue will, in those circumstances, bring admiration too, and the honor and praise that is the hero's due.

Consider Interstate Battery System of America, a privately owned company that markets automotive batteries manufactured by Johnson Controls through a system of local independent distributors. These distributors service thousands of car dealerships and repair shops. Recently the company opened its All Battery Centers, which also sell batteries for electronic and cordless devices. Interstate Battery is owned by Norm Miller, a born-again evangelical who promotes his Christian values throughout the firm, most explicitly in the corporate culture. Headquartered in Dallas, Texas, the company founded the annual Great American Race and sponsors a number of other family-based events. Interstate is seeking to demonstrate godliness in all it does—in the way it treats people as customers, partners and employees. The top leadership shares a vibrant faith, which it openly and courageously shares. That faith colors decision-making and the way that business is conducted: honestly and in trust, towards the goal of serving God.

The motive of charity, like courage, is seen at its most admirable not in the moment of success, but in the moment of failure when, despite grievous loss, a person thinks of the misfortunes of others and strives to remedy them. An interesting example is Aaron Feuerstein, owner and CEO of Malden Mills, whose business suffered a serious setback when his factory in Lawrence, Massachusetts—the small manufacturing town to which the Feuerstein family had devoted their lives for close on a century—burned down in 1995. Despite the loss, Feuerstein continued to pay the wages of his three thousand unemployed workers during the months that it took to rebuild the factory. Many people regard business, he says, "as a battle for profits, which has nothing to do with trying to do good, or what's right on this Earth. That's relegated to when you go home. . . . And if you are so inclined, you could be charitable to others. . . . But I don't think of it that way. I think of it [as I was taught by] my religious Jewish upbringing, that . . . being of service to other people, *mitzvah*, is the greatest good deed one can do." Because of this good deed, Malden Mills was unable to recover from the disaster of the fire and was forced into bankruptcy in 2003. Many would regard this outcome as a proof that charity and business are opposites. But that is to ignore the true nature of virtue, which is not a quick fix that guarantees success, but an engrained state of mind and character, an outlook on the world that turns even failure to good account. Aaron Feuerstein was able to come away from his bankruptcy with a clear conscience, enjoying the unsullied reputation that will permit him to live with this setback. And through his example he has revived people's faith in the American manufacturing economy and has indirectly contributed to its renewal.

Turn now to an illustration of the absence of faith in a business that was otherwise one of the most vivid examples of self-propelled success in recent British history, GEC-Marconi. This company was built from scratch by Arnold Weinstock, born to a Jewish tailor and his wife who had immigrated to London from Poland. Arnold was orphaned at the age of eleven, and thereafter worked his way through life in a spirit of grieving but determined skepticism. His fortunes changed when he married into the Sobell family, also of Polish Jewish origins, and began helping his father-in-law, already head of a multimillion-pound radio business, to establish his company, GEC, as the leading player in the new television market. Arnold Weinstock was formidably intelligent, with a keen eye for accounts, and would let no penny escape his scrutiny. He struck fear into his employees and ruled GEC with a rod of iron as it grew to become a major contractor to the government in military electronics. Arnold had the ear of four successive prime ministers, Labour and Conservative, and by the time the British economy entered a temporary recession under

John Major, GEC was turning a profit of £1 billion a year, with Lord Weinstock, as he had become, hailed as the leading industrialist of his country and as living proof that, underneath the fluctuating surface, the British economy was as fit and competitive as it had ever been.

Arnold Weinstock moved easily in the worlds of his two great loves, which were horses and music, and looked forward to the day when he could hand over his company to his son Simon and retire from the scene. His success had brought him enemies, as had his reputation for thrift and his friendship with leading Conservatives; but everyone who knew him admired him for his wit and recognized the touching streak of sadness that tempered whatever he did. Arnold Weinstock was thrifty, determined and courageous, and the business reflected these qualities. He was also driven by a higher purpose than gain, which was to present Simon, whom he adored, with an empire worthy of him. But family love, however admirable in itself, is no substitute for faith, and when Simon died of cancer at age forty-six, Arnold gave in to despair. The loss seemed meaningless—final proof of the emptiness of human efforts—and it caused Arnold to look back over his years as a businessman with a sense of futility. Unable to continue, he handed over the business, in which he had invested so much careful thought and energy, to a successor who had not the faintest understanding of how it worked and no respect for the internal traditions of the firm. Within three years, thanks to random fragmentation and ill-considered changes of goal, the company had declined in value from £35 billion to £150 million. Arnold watched with sorrow as his life's work was squandered. Only then, seeking consolation for his grief, did he turn to the faith of his fathers, finding peace at last and dying as a liberal but believing Jew, loved and forgiven by everyone who knew him.

The Jewish faith is in fact exemplary in its attitude to commerce, and this helps to explain why Jews down the ages have been able to surmount the trials of persecution and anti-Semitism, so as to be everywhere successful in business. The Talmud holds that the first question to be asked of each of us at the last judgment will be "Were you honest in your business dealings?" The Torah and the Talmud are replete with guidance and examples emphasizing the virtues needed in commerce and the legitimacy of commerce when conducted according to those virtues.

Josh Friedman, CEO and chief marketer of Eleven Wireless, a firm founded in 2001 by three Jewish friends, explains that his principles in business derive directly from the Torah, and that he and his colleagues are constantly interrogating their Jewish faith for commercial guidance. Difficult issues become immediately clearer when brought into this perspective. The sacred texts offer clear counsel on honesty and transparency, on pricing, on relations with employees, and on social and environmental responsibility. By seeking to find the "way of the pious" in all the entanglements of business, Eleven Wireless has built up the confidence of its founders, the loyalty of its staff and the endorsement of its customers and stakeholders. In 2005 it won the Development Stage Company of the Year award for successful enterprise, an honor that it achieved not by aiming at wealth or expansion without regard for others, but by doing business according to Jewish law, recognizing that wealth is rightly created only when rightly used, with due charity towards the needy and the stranger.

Catholic Health Initiatives, coming out of the Benedictine tradition, has made significant strides in promoting workplace spirituality in the decade since its inception as a national system for health care delivery. Based in Denver, Colorado, it operates as a Catholic-inspired company, with over 65,000 employees. Its sixty hospitals, as well as nursing homes and community ministries and centers in nineteen states across the country, allow opportunities for staff prayer and reflection on a daily basis. Catholic Health provides local forums for employees to come together to share what gives meaning to their work, and to articulate the difference they are making in the lives of those they serve. An annual publication called *Sacred Stories* includes testimonies and vignettes about finding spiritual meaning in the exercise of one's daily responsibilities. In-service retreats and days of reflection are provided on a routine basis for staff and physicians as well as board members.

Catholic Health has developed a rich process for assessing core values. It has established a rigorous methodology for setting clear expectations and holding staff accountable for what they do each day. Values-based behaviors are defined in terms of a spirituality tied to sixteen attributes of the company's distinctive culture. Quantitative and qualitative data are collected for each local facility, and also for national staff, to assess ongoing development in cultural attributes. Key priorities in further shaping the desired culture grounded in spirituality are then incorporated into strategic planning efforts and operational performance goals.

Catholic Health is actively attempting to integrate spirituality with the way it does business and the way it delivers health services in its ministry of healing. The challenge is to identify and foster the world of spirit among employees and partners as an integral component of organizational performance. This goal fits cohesively with real measures of success in the health care industry nationally. The use of behavioral metrics for a culture grounded in spirituality helps people recognize that the unity of who they are and what they do is more than meets the eye. Catholic Health celebrates the spirit of work in a way that makes a difference for others. Recognizing staff for the inner self they bring to the workplace enables them to demonstrate humanity and personalized care for individuals with names and faces, rather than just attending to patients with medical conditions.

A telling example of faith and its connection with hope and

charity is William Pollard, chairman of ServiceMaster, which under his leadership has achieved an average annual return to its shareholders of 20 percent. Pollard is articulate on the subject, and also keenly aware of the complex way in which faith acts on a modern economy. His is a business that, from one point of view, is entirely mundane: cleaning toilets and floors, killing bugs, cleaning carpets and so on. But as the poet George Herbert put it, in what was to become a favorite Victorian hymn:

> *A servant with this clause*
> *Makes drudgery divine;*
> *Who sweeps a room as for Thy laws*
> *Makes that and th' action fine.*

That is the ethos of ServiceMaster as William Pollard conceives it. Carved in stone on the wall of his company headquarters in Downers Grove, Illinois, are the four principles that define his company: "To honor God in all we do; to help people develop; to pursue excellence; and to grow profitably." As with Dacor, the first of these rules is by far the most important. By honoring God in your actions, you change them from a routine to a sacrament. And once you see them in that way, you perform them cheerfully, rightly and profitably.

Pollard gives two interesting examples. The first is that of Shirley, an employee of his company and a housekeeper in a 250-bed hospital, who has remained interested in and attached to her cleaning job for fifteen years. Shirley sees her job as an act of service to the patients, and as much an integral part of curing them as the work of the nurses and the doctors. "In a very real sense," Pollard says, recounting his meeting with her, "she was leading me, by talking about her work, her customers and her role in our shared mission." Reflecting on Shirley's pride in her work, he comments:

> Everyone has a fingerprint of personality and potential and
> desire to contribute. When we define people solely in economic

terms, our motivational and incentive schemes tend to become mechanical and manipulative. We try to define a system that will idiot-proof the process, which can in turn make people feel like idiots. *Fortune* magazine recently described the soulless company as suffering from an enemy within, citing Henry Ford's quote as descriptive: "Why is it that I always get the whole person when what I really want is just a pair of hands?"

As William Pollard emphasizes, however, it is the whole person to whom you must relate, be it as employer or employee, as customer or provider, and faith directs you to that whole person, made in the image of the supreme person who rules over all. He interestingly compares the case of Shirley with that of Olga, whom he met in Leningrad (as it then was called) during a trip to the Soviet Union:

> She had the job of mopping the lobby floor in a large hotel which at that time was occupied mostly by people from the West. . . . She had been given a T-frame for a mop, a filthy rag, and a bucket of dirty water. She really wasn't cleaning the floor; she was just moving dirt from place to place. The reality of Olga's task was to do the least amount of motions in the greatest amount of time until the day was over. Olga was not proud of what she was doing. She had no dignity in her work. She was a long way from owning the result.
>
> I knew from our brief conversation that there was a great unlocked potential in Olga. I am sure you could have eaten off the floor in her two-room apartment—but work was something different. No one had taken the time to teach or equip Olga. She was lost in a system that did not care. Work was just a job that had to be done. She was the object of work, not the subject.

Think back to Shirley: what makes her experience of work so different from Olga's? Yes, one was born in Moscow and the other in

Chicago, and their cultures, languages and nationalities were different. But their basic tasks were the same. They both had to work for a living. They both had limited financial resources. One was proud of what she was doing; her work had affected her view of herself and others. The other was not proud, and she had a limited view of her potential and worth.

The difference, I suggest, has something to do with how they were treated in the work environment. In one case, the mission of the firm involved the development of the person, recognizing the employee's dignity and worth. In the other case, the objective was to provide activity and call it work.

Philosophers and theologians will have their own ways of describing the difference between Shirley and Olga. For William Pollard, however, the difference is simple: Shirley, who is treated as a whole person by her work, sees herself in the same way; Olga, who is "just a pair of hands," is even less than a pair of hands—the mutilated remnant of a person, whose work deprives her of any sense of her intrinsic worth. Shirley is honored in her work; Olga is despised. Shirley grows in her work; Olga shrinks. And underlying the difference is the faith that guides ServiceMaster versus the cynical atheism of the communist system.

As in the cases of Tom Monaghan and Rumi Verjee, William Pollard's faith leads to the constant wellspring of hope that brings success and cheerfulness to his company, and also to the acts of charity through which he acknowledges his debt. In his book *The Soul of the Firm*, Pollard brings home the fundamental truth on which all successful enterprise depends, which is that when people join together in an enterprise they create a new person, the firm itself, which is something greater than the sum of its parts. It too has a soul, and if its members honor God, then it too honors God. If its members aim to do good, it too aims to do good. And just as we are more successful in our undertakings if we approach them from a standpoint of faith and trust, so too is a corporation more successful when faith and trust are built into its structure. As the Catholic philosopher Michael Novak has argued, the corporation shows the "working of grace" in the world, just as the individual does: it is called to the higher life, or it can sink to the lower. As a manifestation of human freedom, it is on trial in the world and is called to a life of virtue. This is a point to which I shall return in the final chapter.

Of course, ServiceMaster requires no orthodox faith or any faith at all from its employees. It is, rather, an *expression* of faith: a firm built on a belief in the intrinsic worth of human beings and their work, which has been able to confront and overcome the stigma that so often attaches to the work of the cleaner and the janitor, and to bring true satisfaction to its employees. In this instance we see very clearly what is meant by spiritual capital: namely the long-term investment of trust that is contained in a religious faith, and which enables people freely to elicit the best in each other, however menial the task.

There is another aspect to faith in the workings of a corporation that is usefully brought out by William Pollard in his examples. Of Olga he says, "She was the object of work, not the subject." In other words, in her work she is treated as a thing to be used, like a human broom. Shirley, by contrast, has no such vision of herself. She belongs to a firm that treats her as a willing partner in a common enterprise, extending to her full responsibility for her part in things, and regarding her work as a proof of her individual worth. She is a subject, not an object: which is to say that she gives herself freely to her work and finds herself in it.

This difference between the situations of Shirley and Olga connects directly with the spiritual capital that has been invested in ServiceMaster, and which was entirely absent from the workplace under

Soviet rule. The first of ServiceMaster's rules, to honor God in all we do, actually sets the tone for the other three and defines their content. You honor God by respecting his image, which is the human person. That is the simplest and most direct way of translating the first commandment of religion into a day-to-day policy, and it underlies Christ's own rephrasing of the Ten Commandments: to love God with all your might and all your soul, and to love your neighbor as yourself. The second commandment expresses and follows from the first. In the context of business, this means helping the members of your firm to develop as people—to become free subjects instead of dependent objects, to be fully at one with their work and imbued with a sense of purpose.

The third of ServiceMaster's principles continues the train of thought: when people freely identify with their work and find themselves through it, then the pursuit of excellence follows as a matter of course. Shirley takes pride in her work because it is *her* work, an expression of her free nature. Because she is respected as a person, she respects herself in her work—and that means pursuing excellence. The fourth of ServiceMaster's principles is then automatically satisfied: when the members of a corporation freely and willingly pursue excellence in their work, the result is profitability. And the performance of ServiceMaster under William Pollard's leadership is proof of this.

Notice, however, that profitability comes last among the principles: it is not the primary goal of the company, but the consequence of doing business in the right way, so as to honor God. And this gives us a clue to the significance of spiritual capital in the world today. In the nineteenth century, capitalism had some harsh critics. They did not deny that the industrial revolution had vastly increased the wealth of modern societies, nor did they necessarily agree with Marx that capitalism would enter a terminal crisis. Their concern was to emphasize the social and spiritual condition of the worker who, under the regime of factory production, was turned from a person to a thing, a mere cog in the machine, whose God-given freedom had been stolen from him. Nor was it only socialists who saw industrial capitalism in that way. The same criticism was made from a puritan perspective by John Ruskin, and from the perspective of the Roman Catholic faith by Pope Leo XIII in his celebrated encyclical *Rerum novarum* of 1891. There was a growing consensus that the factory worker was "alienated" in his labor—unable to find himself in it or to express his full humanity.

As we know from subsequent history, it was not capitalism that caused this condition. When socialism arrived on the scene and the state took over the factories, the situation of the worker was in fact worsened. In a socialist economy, everyone is reduced to the condition of William Pollard's Olga, since nobody is honored and freedom is denied. Only in a free economy are people motivated to pursue excellence, and this requires that they be helped to grow and develop in their work. This condition is exactly what is put in place by the spiritual capital on which ServiceMaster draws. The investment was not made yesterday, nor was it made only by the founders and directors of the firm. Like social capital, spiritual capital accumulates through the long-term cooperation of people across generations. It is a deeply settled habit of respect for the divine order of the world, a sediment of worship and prayer, which makes respect for God's creation and respect for people second nature among those who possess it. By emphasizing this capital and bringing it to the fore, ServiceMaster helps all its employees to connect with it in themselves, whether or not they retain any precise religious belief or orthodox habit of worship. The capital investment has already been made—that is the crucial point. The successful firm is the one that knows how to release that investment into the stream of daily business.

Return now to the case of Rumi Verjee. In his long period of struggle he had felt the presence of the helping hand that would one day guarantee success. And this faith in a higher power brought trust in his fellow human beings. When he had sold his franchise in Domino's, he looked at once for another project, forming a partnership with two others in order to buy and develop London's old Royal Brompton Hospital. This was a £120 million project, in which he stood to lose everything he had gained; but faith and hope urged him forward, and the three partners drew up a simple agreement on a single sheet of paper as they ended their meal. One partner was a Muslim, another an orthodox Jew and the third a pious Catholic. The trust that arose between them reflected the teachings of their several faiths, and each knew that cheating would be inconceivable. The spiritual capital on which Rumi Verjee drew in this new adventure had been accumulated over centuries, in three quite different communities under three different historical experiences. But it was still possible to pool this capital and to support each other in taking what was, at the time, an enormous risk. The risk paid off, and Verjee restored his family's fortunes. He recalled the experience that had made this pooling of spiritual resources so easy, which was the sight of Mother Teresa's simplicity and her trust in human goodness. From her charity stemmed both faith and hope. In business as in life, faith, hope and charity are really one.

Students of visionary companies will be aware that vision does not come only from religious faith. Companies can grow around their own "ideology"; or they may turn themselves into "cults," in the manner of Nordstrom, Disney and Wal-Mart—producing their own internal caricature of religion in order to attach their employees heart and soul to the business. They may organize themselves around a secular ethos of service, like Hewlett-Packard, or even, like Procter & Gamble, cultivate a kind of mystique of membership that encourages employees to identify themselves as living in a world apart. It seems to me, however, that all these forms of vision, while they may be productive in themselves, are downstream from faith; they are means to recuperate in a secular and skeptical age some of the spontaneous respect for work, freedom and enterprise that stems from spiritual capital. In other words, they are ways of continuing to draw on a capital investment made over centuries by people who saw business differently—not as a substitute for religion, but as a way in which people could turn God's gifts to an earthly purpose by releasing their collective energies. As we saw from the example of Service-Master, faith in God leads to faith in people; and from that faith, success in business issues of its own accord.

The point is gradually being appreciated in the business world, with many companies sponsoring organizations like Spirit at Work, which seeks to return spirituality to the workplace, and which has established a series of annual awards to recognize those firms that are setting an example. According to recent Gallup polls, 78 percent of Americans today seek spiritual growth, compared with 20 percent in 1994, and 60 percent of executives respond positively to the term "spirituality." The great advantage of a faith-based business is that it can turn these facts to immediate use, by offering without hesitation both the spiritual refreshment that its employees are seeking and a kind of direction that makes the yearning for spiritual growth something more than a New Age fantasy. Even when explicit faith is played down, firms have discovered that they can offer a kind of spirituality in the workplace that effectively transforms what happens there.

Take the case of Elcoteq, Europe's biggest electronic manufacturing service company, headquartered in Luxembourg. Elcoteq recently acquired a factory in Offenburg, Germany, with over 350 employees. Previously, the plant had been owned by various large global telecom companies and went through major restructuring and downsizing as a direct result of the collapsing telecom market. Consequently, the company needed to achieve a rapid turn-around under harsh competitive pressure. The factory had to become profitable and at the same time to decrease prices for existing customers within three years. This was particularly challenging due to a historical employer-union conflict and a demoralized workforce.

Elcoteq decided to manage the turn-around by focusing on spiritual values. Its policies included the cultivation of trustworthiness through a feedback process; the inculcation of respect, encouraging suggestions of the month from all employees; an explicit concern for justice, with new salary models and bonuses; an ethos of service and humility, with Christmas dinner served to a less fortunate group; team spirit, encouraged by forming teams that would be rewarded for winning new customers; family cohesion and family values, supported by a family day for all employees; and so on. Through these measures the factory has achieved outstanding financial results and has won additional customers and business in a highly competitive market. Turnover exceeded the budget by 25 percent and profit doubled. The efficiency of the workforce increased by over 20 percent and the number of employees grew. The employees, having been disgruntled and demoralized before the policy change, now rate their satisfaction in the highest 1 percent of all companies in the comparison group and contribute to the factory's success with an extraordinary and sustained ambition.

Interesting in another way is the Dutch firm of Van Ede & Partners. Like Elcoteq, Van Ede has seen the need of its staff for spiritual values; and like Elcoteq, it has sought to deliver this need without making an explicit faith commitment. But its culture is directly derived from the spiritual legacy of the Netherlands, and it has the effect of clearing the spiritual place into which faith can enter. This is particularly relevant to Van Ede's business, which is that of outplacement—

bringing people and firms into creative relation with each other. Thus Van Ede has introduced meditation and reflection as daily practices in the workplace. Each consultant aspiring to join the company must write a personal autobiography, reflecting on his life and career with a view to making sense of them. The resulting self-analysis is discussed with a psychologist and in dialogue with others, in order to explore the values and meanings that motivate the individual life. Van Ede begins all office meetings with a brief moment of reflection in which employees are asked to empty themselves of everyday thoughts and make contact with a universal power: not prayer exactly, but the posture from which prayer spontaneously emerges. And, as in the great religious tradition from which the culture of the Netherlands grew, singing is all-important for Van Ede, with chorales and spirituals, chants and mantras used to launch the firm's meetings, the employees sometimes managing all four voices of the chorale. The results have been spectacular, with everybody reporting a feeling of lightness and goodwill in their work, as the boundary between work and life first becomes permeable and then dissolves.

A city is built through faith and bears the mark of faith in its churches, its facades and its public buildings. People turn those buildings to new purposes; they may be cared for and repaired; or they may be allowed to crumble. But without them the economy of the city could not grow; nor could future generations, who may have lost the faith that built the city, enjoy the humane and respectful environment that comes from building in the way of faith.

The same is surely true of spiritual capital. It is built through faith, and thereafter remains like the infrastructure of a city, a place in which we can roam, allowing our freedom to express itself, trusting in each other and in the results of our common enterprises. Visionary companies arise, taking up residence in one of the spiritual structures that have been built by previous generations, making "service" or "magic" or "loyalty" their ideology. But these goals depend upon our ability to pursue them, and this ability is there in us because we can draw, like Elcoteq and Van Ede, on a common fund of spiritual capital. In drawing on it we are also learning to emulate the virtues with which it has been associated.

In this chapter I have written of the three theological virtues—faith, hope and charity. In the next chapter I shall show more specific virtues at work in the business environment, and how they too can be amplified and nurtured from this all-important spiritual capital.

4. Hard Virtues: Leadership, Courage, Patience, Perseverance, Discipline

> Great men are they who see that spiritual is stronger
> than any material force, that thoughts rule the world.
>
> *Ralph Waldo Emerson*

SUCCESS DOES NOT USUALLY COME from good luck or random chance. It comes because you are prepared for it and because you have the character that can achieve it. This is true of every walk of life and not just of business. Greek and Roman theories of virtue connected the virtues with practical success—"hitting the target" in Aristotle's simile. On the whole, the Greeks took the approach that I have associated with the hard defenders of capitalism and with its soft opponents: the view that success in action involves courage, fortitude, endurance, discipline—characteristics that we too regard as virtues, but which, we tend to believe, must be tempered by softer passions if they are not to be simply another and more dangerous form of selfishness.

The Greeks were also wary of defining the ideal person in terms of virtues that could be used purely in the pursuit of selfish ends, and they argued that the virtues were incomplete without justice, which is the disposition to pay due regard to others and to satisfy their legitimate demands. To this we should add a whole spectrum of virtues that are "other-directed," such as humility, compassion and forgiveness. The benefit of these softer virtues is not conferred primarily on oneself but on others. In the next chapter I shall show that their altruistic character, far from preventing them from contributing to business success, makes them essential to the development of true entrepreneurship.

In this chapter I shall consider the hard virtues of leadership, courage, patience, perseverance and discipline. There is no doubt that we admire these qualities when we find them in others, and that we wish to possess them ourselves. But how do we acquire them, what exactly do they do for us, and what form should they take?

Leadership

It has become a platitude to say that success requires leadership, and in many ways the platitude is destructive, since it seems to imply that success depends not on you but on somebody else—the leader who will step in and take charge of things. In speaking of leadership as a virtue, however, we are not saying that it lies outside the person whom it benefits. We are saying that it is a quality contained potentially in all of us, a quality that can be developed and realized, so that each of us is able to lead *himself* to his goal. This means that the true leader is also a good follower: he is able to take and give advice, to receive and offer help, to join with others without subduing or alienating them. Reflecting on this, the celebrated management guru Robert Greenleaf developed the concept of "servant leadership." Greenleaf argued that leaders, including corporate bosses, should think of themselves in the first place as servants, devoted to the well-being of those whom they are appointed to lead. Greenleaf took this idea from Herman Hesse's *Journey to the East*, though it is also fundamental to the Roman Catholic faith, which describes the Pope, leader of the Church, as *servus servorum Dei*: the servant of the servants of God. By focusing intently on the needs and aspirations of others, you equip yourself to lead them to your common goal. This cannot be done without a measure of humility—and here we see already how the hard virtues that I discuss in this chapter are deeply and intimately connected with the soft virtues to which I turn in the following chapter. The leader must put his own needs and desires sufficiently out of mind that he can adopt the needs of others as his primary motive.

Greenleaf's *Servant Leadership* was a major influence on Max DePree, CEO of Herman Miller and one of America's best-known business leaders, under whose stewardship Herman Miller advanced to seventh on the Fortune 500 list in terms of profitability (return to investors) and first in productivity (net income generated per employee). DePree found inspiration too in St. Luke's Gospel and the example of leadership that Christ gave to his disciples. Throughout his working life, DePree has addressed his business problems through prayer, and his prayers are less for himself than for the employees under his care. Servant leadership became a part of his faith commitment. Early in his tenure as CEO, DePree convinced the company to introduce an employee stockownership plan so as to share its wealth with its workers. This idea, revolutionary at the time, was intended to benefit the workforce; but it had immediate benefits for the company too, as the employees began to identify more closely with its success. Later, when the company was constantly exposed to hostile takeover attempts, DePree was dismayed by the fact that, in the event of takeover, just a few people at the top were compensated with a "golden parachute." He therefore instituted a system of "silver parachutes" so that all employees would be compensated in case of takeover. This too had a spinoff for the company, DePree discovered, in that it raised the cost of takeover and therefore deterred hostile bids. But the policy wasn't primarily designed to prevent a takeover. It was primarily designed to bring equity. By identifying with his employees in this way, DePree was more effectively equipped to lead them, and in particular to begin the series of innovations that led to Herman Miller's striking successes in the office furniture market.

Reflecting on his career, DePree affirms that "leadership is a function of questions. And the first question for a leader is: 'Who do we intend to be?' Not 'What are we going to do?' but 'Who do we intend to be?'" Leadership, in other words, is a matter of character, not goals. It concerns the way in which you treat others, the comparative value that you place on their and your desires, the values that come first for you and which you refuse to compromise. And in all these things the greatest fund of support is faith.

Some small companies demonstrate leadership on a modest scale, while a few large companies have succeeded because of leadership on a truly global scale. Cargill began 140 years ago as a grain storage facility in the American Midwest. Today it is the largest private company ($90 billion) in the world, with 158,000 employees in 66 countries, providing food, agricultural and risk management products and services to an international market.

Cargill produces and distributes grain, oilseeds and other commodities to manufacturers of food products and animal feed. It provides farm services and stocks to crop and livestock producers, besides working with food manufacturers, services and retailers to supply meat and poultry products and other food and beverage ingredients. What may be less known is Cargill's active development of science-based nutritional ingredients and systems for the food and pharmaceutical industries. The company has also begun to develop and market sustainable products, like ethanol, made from agricultural feed stocks. And since Cargill is such a large-scale player in its markets, it has perfected risk management and financial solutions for its customers.

Today Cargill is a highly diversified global company—no longer just a grain trader. It is one of America's most successful family-owned businesses, though it has experienced its ups and downs over the years. Cargill owes its success to a deep-rooted culture of ethics, innovation and leadership, formed with the spiritual capital of the Presbyterian family that founded the company. In 1865, Cargill established its business practices on the motto "Our word is our bond." In the twenty-first century, Cargill has reaffirmed this pledge by formally adopting a set of "guiding principles"—an ethical standard by which the company does business around the world. Cargill has also committed itself to being a "global leader in corporate citizenship" within the communities where it operates. Citizenship is defined as *total impact* on society and the environment, and for Cargill this includes "responsible business practices; promoting a sustainable environment; engaging our workforce and ensuring their safety; providing a measurable positive impact in our communities."

In 1975 the president of Cargill, Whitney MacMillan, in response to a number of scandals around the world involving businesses in questionable practices and illegal activities, sent all Cargill employees a reminder of their goals and objectives. Saying that integrity had always been Cargill's policy and the basis of its reputation, MacMillan articulated five principles that underscored the spiritual capital on which the company was built:

1. *This means* we have a deep responsibility to conduct ourselves and our business under the highest standards of ethics, integrity, and in compliance with the laws of all countries and communities in which we have been granted the opportunity to perform our services.

2. *This means* should there be a question concerning a particular practice, open discussion will surely resolve the issue. If a practice cannot be discussed openly, it must be wrong.

3. *This means* business secured by any means other than legal, open, honest competition is wrong.

4. *This means* if a transaction cannot be properly recorded in the company books, subject to an independent audit, it must be wrong.

5. *This means* that Cargill does not want to profit from any practice which is immoral or unethical. Should we discover our business

being done in any other than an absolutely proper manner, disciplinary action will be taken.

MacMillan concluded by stating that "a company with a good reputation is a good place to work. Cargill has enjoyed years of a fine reputation built on integrity. We must maintain our honor and self-respect as a basis for our continued growth and pride in the Cargill Companies."

What exactly did Cargill do right that so many others, including many of its primary competitors, did not? Cargill is a private company; it does not typically seek publicity and has even been called a bit secretive. But a telltale *Harvard Management Update* (June 2006) on "The Power of Social Capital" quietly unfolds the Cargill story and discloses the value of its social capital—the informal networks, accumulated know-how, mutual understanding and trust that make an organization effective. This social capital, rooted in the spiritual mores of the founders, is what has paid great dividends for Cargill. They hire people for aptitude and attitude; they train like crazy and have an apprentice program to nurture people; they walk the talk of values; they network to create opportunities for people to share ideas openly; they use decision-making techniques that lead to the adoption of common processes; they make a long-term commitment to their employees; their senior managers keep in touch with the field; and purpose is something that everyone knows and shares. A high purpose has kept Cargill focused for action.

What is remarkable about Cargill is that the high standards of its leadership and the use of social capital rooted in a spiritual definition did not put the company at a disadvantage. Instead of cutting corners, it allowed Cargill to have a leg up and ensured high productivity. This kind of capital may never appear on the balance sheet, but as Cargill has demonstrated, its bottom-line impact is real.

Courage in Business

Perhaps the most eloquent of the hard virtues is courage, the disposition to encounter adversity head-on and strive to overcome it. What does this do for us and what exactly does it involve? Jonathan Ruffer, CEO of Ruffer Investments, a London-based investment agency, has witnessed many shipwrecked businesses among his contemporaries, and is convinced that in nine cases out of ten a lack of courage has been a principal cause. His own success, he believes, is due to acts of bravery founded in faith. Having set up a partnership to manage other people's money, which acquired the old but moribund firm of Rathbones in 1988, Ruffer found himself unable to act in behalf of his clients, since he did not control the money but merely negotiated the terms with those who invested with the firm. He agonized for several years, believing that he was betraying the trust that clients placed in him by not taking advantage of the investment opportunities that he saw. "There is one thing that God has withheld from his creatures, which is knowledge of the future," he says. "To claim that knowledge would be *hubris*. But I have a gift nevertheless, and it is through parleying with my Maker that I came to understand this gift and recognize that I must thank him for it. How do I thank him for his gift? By using it. I needed only the courage to take the first step."

Courage, for Ruffer, is not just an ordinary habit, but a reaching out to God. He left Rathbones and set up on his own, trusting his spiritual intuition. Rathbones took out a legal injunction, preventing him from taking his clients with him for a year. Ruffer had to begin from nothing, and to support his family on hope. He took the bold step of aiming at "absolute return": in other words, investing in such a way as to make money for his clients each year, and not merely to meet the benchmarks that were standard in investment management. In the twelve years of his business, he has averaged a return of 12.5 percent, and his business is now worth £200 million. Almost all his clients left Rathbones to join him as soon as they could, and his reputation in the investment market is now unrivalled.

Courage, Jonathan Ruffer argues, is not a selfish attribute: it is possible only if you are pursuing some wider and more worthy goal. Courage for selfish ends is mere aggression, and when not tempered by reflection and self-criticism it is foolhardiness. Ruffer attributes his understanding of these things to his faith, which has led him to pour the profits of his enterprise into charitable missions in London's East End and into the First Fruits Foundation, which offers hope to the no-hopers of the city. People lose hope because they lose courage, he believes, and they lose courage because they lose faith in themselves, in others and in God. The relief of poverty, drug-dependency, alcoholism and the other ills of a modern city does not come through handouts, but through showing the way to action. And that means giving people a sense that confronting risk is not a thing to be avoided, but on the contrary a thing to be courted—a vocation to which we all are called. Jonathan Ruffer puts the point in his own way:

> Understanding courage means understanding that you are not special, that you are faced each day with decisions that in no way differ from decisions that others face and shy away from. The fact that you take them is something that occurs to you only later. Only looking back at my business, do I have any clear idea that I have been taking those decisions and getting things right. In the day-to-day running of things it is not so much "Be brave!" as "Trust Him," which I do. And this trust brings firmness, certainty and an enormous enjoyment in the human side of business.

The example of Jonathan Ruffer illustrates an important connection between courage and spiritual capital. Those who act bravely are not acting aggressively, as Jonathan points out. They are measuring their strength against an obstacle and considering how to act for the best in the face of it. They are motivated always by a sense of the worthiness of what they do and the rightness of achieving their goal. The great acts of courage that have been witnessed during wartime, in those who have had to endure the privation and suffering of the concentration camp, or in those who have been able to triumph over persecution, are made possible by the belief in the goal, not as something wanted, but as something worthy and noble. This we learn from Solzhenitsyn, and also from Wladyslaw Szpilman's *The Pianist* and from Nijole Sadunaite's *Song in Siberia*, in which a Lithuanian Catholic recounts the sufferings that she endured through faith, and over which she triumphed through the determination to entertain no hatred for people, but only for the sinful system that had trapped them into doing wrong.

This is true too in business. Of course, there is the ordinary motive of pecuniary gain, and it can never be ignored. But, as Ruffer puts it, "the least fulfilling side of my business lies in making very rich people obscenely rich." Far more important is the sense of serving those who have entrusted their savings to him, knowing that they depend upon his wisdom and his courage to bring them a reward.

There are many ways of coming to this kind of courage. But courage lies dormant in our spiritual inheritance, and is awakened by nothing so readily as the "parleying with your Maker" to which Jonathan Ruffer refers. It was the most important part of the human capital that he brought to his business; but it had to be released, and it was released, at last, only because he asked himself what he had done with God's gift to him and discovered that he had not yet done enough.

Faith engenders courage, and also requires it. In an age of skepticism and ridicule it is tempting to hide one's faith, to deny its foundational role in one's life and feelings, and to act as though it were a personal foible, to be revealed only among intimate friends. This temptation is especially strong in the world of business, since business requires daily dealings with people of differing faiths or none, with all of whom a steady flow of affability must be maintained. Yet it is also true that a business founded on spiritual values must sometimes display them, and in modern circumstances this requires courage. This is becoming more the case as secularism spreads in America and a vociferous lobby opposes all public manifestation of religion, mocking or disparaging those who reveal their faith.

Consider the case of Alaska Airlines, a Christian-owned company based in Seattle. The company distributes prayer-cards to its passengers, and openly advertises its faith and calling. This has led to widespread criticism in the media and among the *bien pensants*. Facing up to this tide of factitious anger and ridicule has required courage, and the company has put itself in the line of fire in order to do what it believes to be right. But it has not been damaged, despite the unpleasantness. On the contrary, most people are more ready to trust someone who honestly confesses to his faith and shows that life has for him a real and transcendental meaning, than someone who evades all mention of any foundation to his way of doing business. Hence Alaska Airlines has built up a large fund of passenger loyalty, and, through mergers and acquisitions, has expanded from its roots in McGee Airways, which flew its inaugural service between Anchorage and Bristol Bay in 1932, to a company that now links forty cities in the United States, Canada and Mexico, employing 10,400 people.

Patience

Patience derives from the Latin *pati*, to suffer, and denotes the ability to suffer in pursuit of some higher goal. The impatient person is the one who sacrifices his ends for the sake of his present irritation. At the first obstacle he abandons the pursuit and changes to another. He responds to setbacks with anger, and attracts to himself the hostility of others, for the very reason that he is unable to conceal his impatience with their faults. By contrast, the patient person, faced with an obstacle, trusts in his own ability to overcome it, to think his way around it to the goal. Patience in adversity is one of the great gifts of faith. But it is not the only exercise of this virtue. There is also the ability to keep the goal constantly before the mind when easier options tempt you along other paths.

In the early seventies, Byron Lewis Sr. nurtured the ambition to enter the advertising profession and to be of service to the African American and Hispanic communities by creating a space for them in the gallery of commercial images that were shaping the new America. His attempts to secure a post in an agency were constantly rebuffed, however: at the time, the purchasing power of ethnic minorities was not considered sufficient for the trade to take them into account. Byron Lewis did not renounce his dream. Instead, thirty years ago, he founded his own advertising and public relations agency, UniWorld, devoted to presenting clients to the large and growing market of African and Hispanic Americans. His patience and optimism were rooted in the religious experience of the African American community. As he explains it:

> Black culture is founded on the belief—a religious belief—that good things will come. In my generation, they have. I admire my forefathers because they persevered when there didn't seem to be much opportunity. . . . But we have . . . an obligation to work hard, because that's what this country, with all its faults, offers to people. And what you see in the communities of color is an absolute commitment to hard work . . . [as well as to] strengthening the family and small business development. And I should certainly underscore the religious foundations of many of these people.

Lewis is putting his finger not only on the secret of his own patient search for a niche in the world of advertising, but also on the long-term commercial advantage that has attached to it. As he implies, the ethnic communities of modern America contain a fund of spiritual capital whose potential contribution to wealth creation has been ignored or discounted. From this store came his own faith, and the patient work that is rooted in it. By engaging with the spiritual inheritance of black Americans, Lewis has inspired many to follow his example and to claim their long-overdue place in the wealth-creating society.

Perseverance

Patience is closely related to perseverance, and both belong to *sophrosune*, prudence, in Aristotle's typology of the virtues. The old adage "If at first you don't succeed, try, try and try again" is one that has many applications in business. But tenacity in pursuit of a goal is not the only form that perseverance takes. Equally important is the capacity to hold firm through adversity, to go on doing what you believe to be right, even when nothing seems to be coming of it, and when others are making headway by doing what is questionable or wrong.

This was the situation experienced by McDonald Williams, the CEO and chairman of Trammell Crow Residential, a Dallas-based real estate firm, who has had to face severe downturns in his business life. One such occurred in the early seventies. "What came to me at that time," Williams says, "was probably as close to an epiphany in business as I've ever had, and that is: 'Wait a minute, why did you come? You came here because of the people and the values. Have those things changed? No. External business environments have changed. We're in trouble, but the reasons I came persist, and I can make a difference in this environment.'" Williams survived and prospered, only to encounter another economic downturn in the eighties, when his perseverance was tried to the limit. He watched colleagues lose sleep, suffer marital breakdown and be tempted to do what they shouldn't be doing. But thanks to his faith, he held firm:

> My faith was more relevant to my business in tough times than anything else because then your values really were square in your face. Are you going to live by them or not? Are you going to look beyond the moment for a longer time frame? Who are you? Are you just your job? Are you just your career? Or are you just your reputation? Or are you just your net worth? [Those things] are important to me, I can't deny that. But I think faith helped me, in that moment, to have perspective.

These words make it clear that perseverance is not just a superficial doggedness of character. It is rooted in the depth of the soul, in the very self-conception of the person, governing how he responds to the questions asked by the face in the mirror. "To thine own self be true," says Polonius, "and it must follow, as the night the day, thou canst not then be false to any man." Faith, which is truth to God, is also truth to self. And from that truth, endurance and perseverance follow.

Discipline

Discipline is involved in all the other virtues that I have discussed in this chapter. But it is never better displayed than when others are trying to undermine your courage and resolve, and assuming that you will eventually break. This has been the situation of the talented British architect Quinlan Terry, who has dedicated his life to the cause of classical architecture, in opposition both to the socially disastrous schemes for collective housing initiated by the modernists in Europe, and to the zoning practices that have led to the tragic decline of American cities.

Terry was born into the milieu of London's Hampstead suburb during the war, the child of atheist, socialist and progressive parents who refused to have him baptized. His parents were delighted with his choice of career, since they saw architecture as the expression of modernist values, devoted to building a brave new world in which reason would triumph over superstition. While studying at the Architectural Association in London, however, Terry was converted simultaneously to classicism and to Christianity. In both he saw the marks of a profound discipline, the one inscribing spirit into stone, and the other turning stony hearts towards the spirit. He studied the architecture of the past, became skilled at drawing, designing and perceiving the classical forms, and longed to try his hand at building in this disciplined way. But the Architectural Association, a stronghold of modernism, would not allow him to graduate on the strength of his designs. Only by submitting modernist plans could he obtain the qualification. This was an early sign of the bigoted opposition that Terry has confronted throughout his career.

He joined the office of Raymond Erith, last remnant of the once great London classical school, taking over the practice when Erith died in 1973. Then he began to face up to his isolation at a time when commissions were hard to find and when the modernists, who had the ear of government and the planning officials, were determined that all public commissions should be theirs. At every point in Terry's career the modernist establishment, including powerful figures like Richard Rogers and Norman Foster, sought to thwart him, denouncing his designs and preventing him from obtaining public commissions. Through long years of hardship he persevered, nevertheless, deriving strength from his Christian faith:

I see parallels at every point between the classical tradition in architecture, and the Christian faith. Both ask us to turn from ephemera and fix our eyes on what endures. Both require discipline, self-denial, contempt for fashion. Both put others before self, and the long-term perspective before the short-term view. Both impress on us the shortness and uncertainty of our earthly life. But because I believe in eternal glory thereafter, for those who trust in Christ, it has not been important to me to pursue worldly success. When the modernists have gained a project that I bid for, I accept this as a sign that God had not intended it for me. They mock my faith but it is they and not I who evangelize. All glory for the modernists belongs in this world, and therefore they invest all their energies in imprinting the image of their spiritual emptiness wherever they can. I like to think that by investing in the next world, I free myself from conflict in this one.

Terry's few commissions led to buildings that were mocked in the architectural press, although greatly loved by clients and by the general public. Terry's practice slowly grew, coming to public attention with the development in 1984 of a large area of the London suburb of Richmond, fronting the Thames. This complex of classical buildings, arranged on a grassy bank above the river, has become one of the most popular tourist attractions in London, and has never ceased to be denounced in the professional journals and ridiculed by those who could not hope to emulate its craftsmanlike finish and popular appeal. Even when clients have sought out Terry as architect for a plan already agreed upon, the modernists have lobbied against him. They caused the planning officers to reject his design for the Brentwood Roman Catholic cathedral in Essex—a building he was able to construct only after appealing against the decision. (The cathedral is now the most popular building in Brentwood.) With surpassing arrogance, Foster and Rogers even wrote to the deputy prime minister asking him to call in Terry's designs for an extension to the Chelsea Military Hospital—designs which had been commissioned by the hospital and accepted by the planners.

Terry's quiet and modest persistence in the face of this unremitting malice has been an inspiration to others, notably to the Luxembourgian architect Léon Krier, who has overseen the Prince of Wales's model village of Poundbury on the outskirts of Dorchester, and also to the growing number of classicists in America, where Terry has been responsible for developments in downtown Williamsburg, Virginia, for the Colonial Williamsburg Foundation. From impoverished beginnings he has built up a successful practice expressive of his faith, producing buildings that are as disciplined and unobtrusive as he is.

Terry's success has not been merely his own, therefore. He has shown how to get away from the tyrannical style, short-lived products and inhuman plans that have done such damage in our cities, by designing humane environments in which people can live, work and develop as social and spiritual beings. He and Léon Krier have inspired the New Urbanism movement in the United States, which now has over a thousand building projects to its credit. The movement is part of a growing reaction against the ideas of planning associated with Le Corbusier and the Bauhaus, which many blame for the socially and aesthetically disastrous developments of the 1960s. Like the socialist theories that inspired them, the architectural nostrums of Le Corbusier and the Bauhaus were based on purely secular ideas of human fulfillment, and were both collectivist and despotic, in the manner of the communist state. Hygiene, cleanliness and the provision of physical needs dictated the forms of those "machines for living in" that Le Corbusier imposed by fiat. And people became cogs in those machines, like William Pollard's Olga in the machinery of the communist state. Not surprisingly, the inmates of the Corbusian suburbs around Paris have now rebelled and given violent vent to their rage against their imprisoning environment. Terry believes that by building for the human spirit we enable people to grow into their environment and to make it a home. By building according to the principles of classicism we build for the greater glory of God and also for the greater happiness of his creatures.

The examples in this chapter have, I hope, illustrated the way in which faith does not merely provide the solid foundation on which virtues are built, but also irradiates the actions that result from it, so as to imbue them with a warmth and humanity that entirely refutes the leftist view of business enterprise as a "cutthroat" business in which monsters fight to the death over the bodies of their victims. Wealth creation is a natural and cooperative process, which needs courage, perseverance, patience and discipline only because these are needed in all honorable actions and are the ingredients of true human success.

5. Soft Virtues: Justice, Compassion, Forgiveness, Gratitude, Humility

> With malice toward none, with charity for all, with
> firmness in the right as God gives us to see the right ...
>
> *Abraham Lincoln*

I T IS NOT DIFFICULT TO UNDERSTAND the place of the hard, masculine virtues in the conduct of a modern business. Courage is an essential part of risk-taking; perseverance and discipline are the *sine qua non* without which no one can rise by his own efforts to a position of prominence in any field of human endeavor. And when we look back at the writings of the Greeks and Romans, we find these masculine virtues at the very core of their thinking. They are the dispositions that lead to "success in action," as Aristotle put it: the strengths that serve to make purpose something more than an idle dream.

We, however, heir to some two thousand years of Christian civilization and brought up in a religion that makes love and forgiveness central to its message, are apt to look askance at those tough old virtues. They are all very well in their place. But that place is not where the heart is. They are useful in obtaining our short-term objectives. But peace of mind and solace of the soul come in another way, through the softer and more feminine virtues of compassion, love and forgiveness. And these, we are apt to think, are essentially domestic, stay-at-home virtues. We do not parade them in the marketplace outside, for they have no business there. Indeed, in that harsh and competitive world they would serve merely to tie our hands and give the advantage to our more ruthless competitors.

That is the thought which underlies much of the leftist criticism of the capitalist system itself. The market economy, it is said, is based on self-seeking and private interest. Introduce compassion and it will fall apart—the price mechanism just will not stand for it. The essence of the capitalist economy is the Darwinian struggle for survival, and the failures must go their way to extinction if the whole process is to work. To go along with this, to accept the capitalist economy as the final solution to all our economic problems, is to commit ourselves to a morality of success, and to condemn the failures. It is to create a world without compassion, in which only the toughest can thrive.

In this chapter I set out to show the falsehood of this charge. Not only is capitalism compatible with the soft virtues; it actually requires them. They have a place in business that is every bit as important as their place in ordinary domestic life, and they make their own often surprising contribution to business success. Furthermore, they constitute the most valuable part of our spiritual capital, and show in the clearest possible way that spiritual enterprise is, or ought to be, at the heart of the free economy.

First, however, we must remind ourselves of a principle that has governed the argument of this book throughout: Profit is not always the aim of business, and sometimes by aiming at it we lose it. This is the message that we have learned from visionary companies. But it is a message that needs to be clearly stated. The economic well-being of a society, Adam Smith pointed out, arises not because we aim at it, but because we are intently aiming at other things, which generate our common prosperity by "an invisible hand." Something similar is true of a company. Its well-being depends on profitability. But often, by seeking at all costs to be profitable, we destroy the conditions on which profitability depends. We alienate our workforce or the local community; we destroy incentive and undermine the workplace as a forum for communal life; we become locked in old and once profitable ways long after the competition has made them unprofitable; and so on. The story has been told many times and in many ways. But the essence is simple: success in a market economy does not come because you aim at it; success comes because you have found your ecological niche and can flourish there by doing your own valuable thing. And doing your own thing must have a social, moral and spiritual dimension if it is to attract the loyalty and commitment of the people with whom and for whom you do it.

Biologists have shown how altruistic strategies benefit the gene pool of the organism that exhibits them. The lioness's willingness to sacrifice herself for her cubs is a survival strategy proved in the stern furnace of evolution, and the willingness of bees to die in defense of the hive is one reason for the long-term success of their species. I do not say that human altruism is in any way as simple as the biological strategies that go by that name, yet it is similar in its contribution to our long-term success. Compassion may have looked like a weakness to Nietzsche, but a society without it will sooner or later founder on the reef of its own heartlessness, as the Soviet Union foundered when all trust was at last withdrawn and universal suspicion set everyone against their neighbor. Forgiveness may seem like a recipe for failure in a world where we compete for scarce resources; but it is the only known solution to human conflict, and the one who can forgive is the one whose wounds are never fatal. Humility is not a virtue that you expect to find in the cut-and-thrust of big business; but the humble person who confesses his faults and duly atones for them is the one best equipped to manage defeat, to accept his losses and to overcome the setbacks that are the routine cost of doing business.

Justice

Before considering the soft virtues, it is worth returning briefly to the ancient idea of justice, which Aristotle and others emphasized as the cardinal virtue, uniting success in action with friendship and right dealings towards others. It is one of the longstanding libels against capitalism, ossified into a "theory" by Karl Marx, that the capitalist "exploits" the workers whom he employs, and that all profit is purchased by injustice. The overthrow of the labor theory of value, the recognition of the role of the entrepreneur and risk-taker, and the development of capital theory have all helped to refute those old and resentful pictures of capitalism. Most of all, thanks to the work of the Austrian and Chicago economists, we now have a much clearer picture of the role of enterprise in a free economy. Enterprise is a cooperative venture, founded in contract, in which rewards are distributed according to the risks undertaken and responsibilities incurred, and in which every member has an interest in according to others their due. In other words, justice is the internal binding principle of an enterprise, and where it is absent the enterprise is in jeopardy. This is not to say that all enterprises deal justly with their employees, or that there are not deep-seated conflicts in the workplace. It is to say, rather, that a firm, as a cooperative enterprise, depends upon just dealings. Injustice is precisely what brings cooperation to a quick end.

But what about the firm's dealings with the surrounding society, with neighbors and competitors and strangers with whom it has no contractual or business deal? This is an area where spiritual capital makes itself vividly known. An illustrative example is that of J. Irwin Miller, the founder of the Cummins Engine Company, a firm that designs, manufactures, distributes and services power technologies, including fuel systems, controls, air filtration, emission solutions and electrical power generation. Headquartered in Columbus, Indiana, Cummins now serves customers in 160 countries through a network of company-owned and independent distributors. Income of $55 million on sales of nearly $10 billion in 2005 put it in the Fortune 500.

Miller, who died in 2004, belonged to the Disciples of Christ, a denomination that emphasizes the need to bear witness to Christ in all one's actions, and to conduct one's life as a form of discipleship.

He set up the Cummins Engine Company on the lines required by his faith, motivated by an ideal of just dealings that distinguished him from many of his competitors in the field. Thus in the 1930s Miller supported the formation of a union at Cummins, an idea that was anathema at the time. Later, in the 1970s, he shut down the Cummins factory in South Africa when the regime would not permit racial integration in the workplace. Even in retirement he risked controversy by supporting the Cummins management in their decision to extend benefits to domestic partners of employees. And throughout his long years building up the company, Miller adhered to the principle that Cummins should be actively improving the communities in which its employees worked and lived. He devoted his fortune to sponsoring outstanding buildings in Columbus; and although his tastes would not endear him to Quinlan Terry, whom I described in the last chapter, his sponsorship has endeared him to many in Columbus, since it has put the city on the map and inspired a resurgence of civic spirit in its residents.

Miller was also known through his activities in the National Council of Churches, which he helped to found in 1950, becoming its first lay president and working to put the assembled churches behind the Civil Rights movement, so that the council became one of the ten sponsors of the historic 1963 March on Washington. Miller saw this work in behalf of the wider demands of justice as continuous with the pursuit of justice towards his own employees. At many points in his career he was prepared to put justice before profit, and was rewarded with the loyalty and commitment of his workforce. It is precisely on account of this commitment that Cummins was able to obtain and maintain its leading position in the market it serves, and the firm remains today a vivid illustration of the way in which faith-based business generates both loyalty and leadership.

The example of Cummins illustrates how justice in the workplace spills over into a more general posture, defining the place of a firm in the surrounding community and in the world as a whole. But justice is a distant and impartial outlook on the world, and does not yet require those partial and suffering attitudes that are so often enjoined on us by faith. Compassion, forgiveness and humility are difficult states of mind. We call them virtues because we find them admirable and often marvel at the people who are guided by them in the trials of life, but we know too—without necessarily being able to put this knowledge into words—that such people have a recourse that will serve them well. These qualities are not easily acquired, however. I do not deny that atheists and skeptics may be every bit as compassionate, humble and forgiving as people of faith. But in cultivating these virtues they draw, like the rest of us, on an accumulated store of spiritual capital that they did not themselves create. Compassion and forgiveness have been taught by religious texts and examples; humility has been fortified by worship and prayer. And it is often the experience of these qualities in ordinary God-fearing people that motivates us to be like them and to amend our lives.

An Unforgiving Businessman

Nicholas van Hoogstraten began his business career at age seventeen, selling his stamp collection for £1,000 and investing in property in the Bahamas. His one interest was to make money, and with astuteness and foresight he was able to sell his Bahamas properties and invest in the British housing market, just before the property boom. At age twenty-two he was Britain's youngest millionaire, with a reputation for ruthlessness towards his tenants and business rivals, and an ability to overcome all opposition by the sheer force of his personality. He was a caricature of the Nietzschean tycoon as Ayn Rand had painted him, and corresponded exactly to the left-wing vision

of the capitalist as a person ruthlessly pursuing his own profit without regard for any interests but his own. By buying cheap and selling
dear, he played the property market to his own satisfaction and without compassion for the "scum," as he called them, whose tenancies
he would abruptly bring to an end—if necessary by intimidation. And
year upon year the profits soared, all accruing to him, for there was no
one else involved: a corporation, after all, is a partnership with others, and for van Hoogstraten others did not count.

Van Hoogstraten had a weakness, however, which was that he
could not forgive. If someone owed money, he had to pay, whatever
his situation. If someone had set himself up as a rival, he must be
punished, whatever the justice of his case. In the 1960s, incensed by a
rabbi who refused to pay an alleged debt, van Hoogstraten launched
a grenade attack on the rabbi's house. For this he spent four years in
jail, a bitter experience that deprived him of the enjoyment of his millions. He emerged from prison with the intention of becoming utterly
secure from all intrusion so as to enjoy his millions on his own terms
and without accommodating others. He built himself a vast mansion
in which to house his extensive art collection and dominate his own
little corner of England. Unfortunately, the house was built across a
right-of-way used by ramblers. Unable to sympathize or to forgive
their intrusion, van Hoogstraten lived in his house like a tiger in a
cage, snarling at every passerby, attacking and molesting his stream
of unwanted visitors and constantly at loggerheads with the law.

Then, in 2000, he fell out with a business rival, Mr. Raja, who
had made the mistake of joining him in a deal and had taken what
he assumed to be his share of the proceeds. Again van Hoogstraten,
unable to see his way to forgiveness, sought punishment instead.
Mr. Raja was killed by two hired henchmen, and in due course van
Hoogstraten was convicted of manslaughter and sentenced to ten
years in jail. Later the verdict was overturned and van Hoogstraten

was released, only to face a civil suit from Mr. Raja's family, in which he was held to be responsible for the death. His property is now under sequestration by the court as he fights to deny compensation to Mr. Raja's family.

You could call that business success if you like: after all, van Hoogstraten is still a millionaire of sorts. But he is condemned to hide his property from the law; he has lost years of his life in prison; and his reputation has been so thoroughly destroyed that he can do nothing with his property that will attract either sympathy or affection from others. He is sitting on a sterile asset that is as immovable and useless as the mausoleum with three-foot-thick walls that he has built for himself in his mansion. Indeed, he is already living in that mausoleum, chanting his Randian mantra that "the purpose of wealth is to put oneself on a pedestal."

The Forgiving Businessman

It is instructive to return here to the case of Jonathan Ruffer, which I considered in the last chapter. When Ruffer left the partnership that he had established, it was with the intention of behaving perfectly. He did not contest the injunction that his partners laid on him, which deprived him of his clients and forced him to start from nothing. Nor did he try to obtain from the partnership anything that was not strictly owed to him under contract. One of the terms of his contract, however, was an option—which he had not yet exercised—to acquire shares worth close on a million pounds for a nominal sum. This was part of his remuneration, and it could be withheld only on grounds of "gross misconduct." So his partners alleged gross misconduct and refused to transfer the shares. Jonathan Ruffer felt the injustice of the charge and knew that if he sued, the charge would be struck down by the courts and the shares would be his. He decided not to sue but instead to study forgiveness. For Ruffer the Lord's Prayer, through which we seek forgiveness and which commands us to forgive in turn, is the true guide to human conflict. By reflecting on this prayer and all the blessings that had been heaped on him, Jonathan Ruffer came quickly to see that forgiveness would be the way to renew his own feelings of hope, to take courage for the future, and to begin his new life with a clean and untroubled conscience. It was far more appropriate to behave correctly, and to seek God's forgiveness for any anger that he might feel, than to seek vengeance for a wrong.

Understood in this way, forgiveness is probably the most important part of our spiritual capital. Not only does it undo the knot of conflict; it sets us always on a new path, and so releases the energy and self-confidence that are dammed up and turned against themselves by anger and resentment. Forgiveness is not just a state of mind; it is a process. The forgiving character is the one in whom that process is constantly engaged, both for others and for himself. This is the truth encapsulated in those exemplary words of the Lord's Prayer: "Forgive us our trespasses, as we forgive those who trespass against us." The Koran too, though it permits retribution for a wrong, insists that the one who endures a wrong with fortitude and forgives it achieves a higher state of grace (42, v. 43).

Now it is much easier to forgive if the person who has wronged you acknowledges his fault and strives to make amends for it. In these circumstances, forgiveness is the endpoint of a moral dialogue in which each treats the other as a fully responsible and accountable being, and respect and liking are restored. This process can be observed in all the day-to-day quarrels of human life; and the big-hearted person is the one who can transfer the process to the great and hurtful wrongs that might otherwise threaten to destroy all possibility of respect, affection or love: the person who can forgive his adulterous wife, his treacherous friend or his prodigal son.

This is not what the virtue of forgiveness amounts to, however. To possess the virtue is to be capable of going beyond that day-to-day transaction, not merely by transferring it to the great wrongs, but by being able to forgive the person who does not acknowledge his wrong, who is determined to seize the advantage and who perhaps even rejoices in your affliction. In domestic life we do not often encounter this kind of person: those who live together in domestic arrangements have an interest in restoring affection. In business, however, as in all activities that bring us into relationship with people whose emotions are withheld from us, we are constantly exposed to indifference—to a personal self-seeking that disregards its victims. And this is the core of the accusation made against capitalism. This attitude of indifference, it is said, is encouraged by the free-market economy. It is precisely by being indifferent to others that we create the free competition through which the capitalist economy advances. In such a system there is no place for forgiveness: it is a dysfunctional residue of emotions that belong to another age and a slower way of doing things.

If that view were true, then we would expect the capitalist economy to be one great predatory tussle, in which people compete as though in a "state of nature," seizing what they can without regard for others. Nobody can deny that the predators exist and they take their toll. But they are essentially intruders or vandals into the market—parasites who seek a rent from other people's labor, and who disturb the normal course of human conciliation. They create the conditions in which the virtue of forgiveness is put to the test.

A case in point is that of John H. Tyson, CEO and chairman of Tyson Foods. In its own words, Tyson Foods strives "to be an honorable and faith-friendly company; to serve as stewards of the animals, land and environment entrusted to us; to earn consistent and satisfactory profits for our shareholders and to invest in our people, products and processes; to operate with integrity and trust in all we do; to honor God and be respectful of each other, our customers, and our stakeholders." This has been the philosophy of Tyson Foods since its founding, and the strong faith-based ideology of the firm has helped it to become the world's largest multi-protein producer, employing more than 120,000 people across the United States and Mexico. John Tyson proudly says, "We don't have employees, we have team members"; and his corporation follows a charter of employees' rights designed to place mutual respect at the very center of the business. It was inconceivable to John Tyson that his workforce should rise against him, or that it should set out to ruin him. But he reckoned without the lawyers. The Association of Trial Lawyers of America has become what is probably the biggest predator of other people's property in the history of mankind. Thanks to the American provisions for "class actions" in tort, it has been able to raise enormous fees for its members by systematically preying on corporations who can be portrayed to some gullible jury as the big exploiters of vulnerable people. Indeed, the left-wing caricature of the capitalist corporation has been useful to no one more than the prototypical American megarich lawyer, who uses it in order to pillage the profits that he could not earn by honest labor.

Allegations were made in 1999 that illegal immigrants were recruited by and employed at some of Tyson's plants; these allegations led to a criminal indictment, of which the corporation was ultimately acquitted. While the trial proceeded, however, lawyers were able to seize on the allegations in order to create a class action, based on the premise that immigrant workers had been imported precisely to lower the wages of indigenous workers, who were therefore entitled to compensation. The lawyers, tempted by profit, tempted Tyson's workforce in turn. The class action suit was brought on behalf of all persons legally authorized to be employed by Tyson Foods at its facilities throughout the United States for a four-year period. And the action took its course. The result was first a pitiless assault on the reputation of Tyson Foods in the media (with Tyson featuring in the top ten "criminal companies" nominated by Corporate Crime Watch), and eventual bankruptcy for John Tyson and his company.

How does one recover from such a blow—losing everything on an unjust charge and in the face of a collective betrayal by those whom one had regarded as one's dependants and friends? The answer is forgiveness. John Tyson studied all the ways in which his team could be forgiven for yielding to a temptation that he had not foreseen. He came to see that the temptation was really an intrusion from outside, that the real predator was not one bound to his firm by any relation of trust, and that he was presented with an opportunity to clear his mind of resentment and begin again. And by forgiving his team, he was reconciled to them. Within a short while he had refinanced his business and returned to his dominant position in the market.

In such an example we see how forgiveness promotes the return to normality and the defeat of a hostile intrusion. Far from being a weakness, it is a strength, underpinning the determination to surmount misfortune andh permitting the renewal of enterprise. Had John Tyson not been able to forgive, had he lapsed into bitterness and resentment, there is no doubt that his business would never have recovered. As it is, he re-entered the market and also helped to restore the economic equilibrium that the lawyers had briefly disturbed.

The Compassionate Business

In 1976, Professor Muhammad Yunus, head of the Rural Economics Program at the University of Chittagong in Bangladesh, began to examine the possibility of designing a credit delivery system to provide banking services targeted at the rural poor. The Grameen Bank Project (Grameen means "rural" or "village" in the Bangla language) came into operation with the objective of extending banking facilities to poor men and women, so as to eliminate their exploitation by moneylenders and create opportunities for self-employment for the vast multitude of unemployed people in rural Bangladesh. The hope was to bring the disadvantaged, mostly the women from the poorest households, within the fold of an organizational format that they can understand and manage by themselves, and to replace the age-old vicious circle of "low income, low savings, low investment" with the virtuous circle of "low income, injection of credit, investment, more income, more savings, more investment, more income." In other words, the idea was to stimulate wealth creation in the spirit that I have been examining in this book: by releasing the creative potential of people who have hitherto been given no opportunities to thrive.

The research demonstrated its strength in Jobra (a village adjacent to Chittagong University) and some of the neighboring villages during 1976–1979. With the sponsorship of the central bank of the country and support of the nationalized commercial banks, the project was extended to Tangail (a district north of Dhaka, the capital city of Bangladesh) in 1979. With the success in Tangail, the project was extended to several other districts in the country. In October 1983, the Grameen Bank Project was transformed into an independent bank by government legislation. Today, Grameen Bank is owned by the rural poor whom it serves. Borrowers of the bank own 90 percent of its shares, while the remaining 10 percent is owned by the government.

The Grameen Bank Project is being copied and extended around the poorest parts of the world, and illustrates the way in which compassion, far from tying the hands of businessmen, enables them to unlock the creative potential of the person whom they help. The scheme of microcredit without collateral—in other words, credit in which all the risk is with the lender—lies outside the boundaries of traditional banking practice and has no foundation other than compassion for and trust in another human being. But the business immediately began to grow, and as of 2004 it had provided funds to over four million borrowers.

The project could be cited as a paradigm of business innovation. But it is also one that unlocks a vast fund of spiritual capital in the ordinary Muslims who have entered the scheme. These are people who, because of their inheritance, respond to trust by offering trust, and receive compassion not as an insult but as an invitation to better themselves. Decades of unemployment and dependency were cast aside just as soon as the spiritual taps were opened. Moreover, by unlocking the creative potential of its 4 million borrowers, the Grameen Bank has enabled the creation of countless assets that would not otherwise have existed. It has catalyzed the creation of real wealth from nothing save the human desire for it.

Just before the Grameen Bank Project was launched, an American Christian initiative took steps in the same direction. It happened that one Sunday in 1972, Alfred Whittaker, recently made president of Bristol-Myers, heard a sermon in which the pastor outlined the need for an organization that would help the poor in developing countries to create jobs. Whittaker, impressed by what he heard, quit his job, sold his house and founded Opportunity International, a nonprofit organization that would lend money and offer advice, oversight and technical education to new entrepreneurs among the poor in developing countries. Most of the loans, like those of the Grameen Bank, fall between the local equivalent of $50 and $800; in 1994, Opportunity International gave out 24,000 of such loans and generated 64,000 jobs. It now works in Latin America, Asia, Africa and Eastern Europe, with fundraising and organizing branches all over the world. It describes itself as a Christian ecumenical organization, motivated by Jesus Christ's call to serve the poor, while serving women and men of all beliefs. It is one of the most striking examples of wealth creation through enterprise that I know, and a clear proof that the most important input into such a venture is not financial but spiritual capital.

Compassion for the poor and needy is only one form that human sympathy can take; the command to love our neighbor as ourselves in fact reaches much further, and it is a command that demands elucidation. "Who is my neighbor?" asks the skeptic, and it is to this question that Christ's parable of the Good Samaritan was addressed. The temptation is to reply "anyone and everyone." But this is a reply that, because it demands too much of us, excuses even more. A command that we cannot fulfill is one that we disobey with an easy conscience. This is why Christ told the parable of the Good Samaritan: not merely to argue against the ethnic and religious prejudices of his contemporaries, but in order to point out that the object of compassion is this person, here and now—the one whom you come across and whose need calls out to you. The New Testament ideal of charity—*agape*—is a form of love. I cannot love the abstract and universal stranger, but I can attend with love to the wounded person who lies in my path.

This kind of compassion also has its role in business, and it is sustained by faith. An interesting example is provided by the case of the Tomasso Corporation, a medium-sized, privately owned company in Quebec that specializes in the production of brand-name frozen dinners and hors d'oeuvres sold in Canadian, U.S. and Mexican markets. The company was founded seventy years ago by Giovanina di Tomasso and based on her popular Italian-style restaurant in Montreal. In the 1950s the business quickly expanded, and in the early 1980s it won a large contract with the giant food retailer Costco. The Tomasso Corporation approached the businessman

Robert Quimet for a capital investment to finance further expansion. Quimet's holding company acquired 100 percent of Tomasso and he became chairman and sole shareholder.

Tomasso continued to grow in the 1990s, but rapid growth also stretched the workforce. New management styles were put in place; old managers left and new ones replaced them. Modern food-processing facilities were added at a new location and the workforce became unionized. Management-employee relations entered a period of strain. With key managers exiting and culture changes imminent, Quimet realized that he needed a new approach in order to rebuild relations with key customers and at the same time deal with pervasive problems of employee morale and productivity.

Quimet sorely wanted to connect his faith and his vocation. For him, deep piety as a Roman Catholic and a disciplined economic approach to managing could no longer run along parallel tracks. He started experimenting with various management practices that would harmonize spiritual values with the demands of productivity. However, sacred ideals proved difficult to fuse with the pressing demands of the workplace. While compassion has an evident place in private life, it can seem remote in the workplace, crowded out by the press for efficiency, short-term profits, accountability, competitiveness, productivity and general tough-mindedness.

Nevertheless, Quimet still thought these two worlds needed to be harmonized. As in the parable of the Samaritan, the object of compassion was here before him in the workplace: the people who had been put into relation with him by the workings of Providence. The demand was for specific management practices that would make sympathy a fully operational part of the business, contributing in its own way to the goals of the firm without undermining its productivity. In other words, the need was to operationalize the spiritual and the economic dimensions of business life. This became the particular focus at Tomasso. Quimet took a sabbatical to write *The Golden Book*, developing and later implementing an approach that everyone in the firm now calls "Our Project" (*Notre Projet*).

Specific management practices commended to the entire management team include: follow-up with employees, even those who have been dismissed; moments of silence; time for contemplation; testimonial speakers; a silence room; annual one-on-one conversations with all employees; service to needy communities; and service and gifts to poor persons—all these initiatives to be accompanied by reflection on the experience. In other words, work relations have been rebuilt as relations of *agape*, not in order to convert the workforce to Quimet's faith, but in order to exemplify that faith as a lived experience.

Like most visions of any real consequence, this dream was not easy to translate into reality. Initial resistance came from fear of proselytizing as well as from social awkwardness and the dislike of being patronized. Only gradually were the practices accepted. Eventually, however, they were not just accepted but extolled by the workforce. Over the years, they have contributed to the development of a unique organizational culture. These practices have served to carry spiritual values into the workplace, where they are received not as dogmas but as the natural voice of human kindness. Today the effect of the new corporate culture is measured and attested in annual worker and customer satisfaction surveys.

Humility

Humility is the most exacting of all virtues, for it requires us constantly to look on ourselves from outside, to judge our own actions as others would judge them, and to acknowledge our faults and failures. It is not surprising to find no equivalent in Aristotle's or Cicero's list of virtues. But it is fundamental to the Christian vision and to the character of Jesus. And it is, I believe, the virtue that is most necessary to us as we strive to come to terms with the global economy, in which people of many faiths are called upon to set aside their differences and cooperate, though without throwing away what is most precious to them, which is their spiritual inheritance.

Millard Fuller had everything: a lovely educated wife, Linda, two beautiful children, the house of his dreams, and a business that he had built up to become a self-made millionaire at age twenty-nine. But his business occupied all his time; making money became the dominant goal of his life, and his marriage began to suffer. Instead of Fuller leading his business, the business was leading Fuller, and leading him further and further from domestic happiness. His wife went from their home in Georgia to New York, to visit a pastor that the couple had known. Linda Fuller recalls: "By the time Millard came to New York, it was like death walked in the door. He realized we were in crisis. I knew I wanted our marriage to work, but I didn't see how that could happen with him working all the time."

The couple walked the streets of New York, talking out their fears and confusions, and ended up sitting on the steps of St. Patrick's Cathedral. Quite suddenly they found themselves sharing their hopes for the future. "On the taxi ride back to the hotel," Linda recalls, "we both felt like God was talking to us and that we should devote our lives to Christian work. The next morning we hailed a taxi and the driver said, 'Congratulations, you're riding in a brand new taxi no-one has ridden in.' We felt it was a sign we were on a brand-new adventure."

Millard and Linda sold everything, gave the proceeds to the poor, and set out to lead a life of humble service to others. At first Millard worked in an African American college, using his business sense to obtain money for the school. Then they went to live in a small Christian community, Koinonia Farm, near Americus, Georgia. It was here that Millard received his calling, in the form of an idea for low-income housing. "While people had been building houses for thousands of years," he relates, "and often with the help of neighbors, no one seemed to be building houses as an expression of God's love. It was too big for any one group. Jews, Christians or Muslims, we would welcome anyone, whoever wanted to participate."

The Fuller family of six moved to Zaire, to test their housing model in a developing country, and their three years there were marked by such success that they decided to propagate their idea around the world. Habitat for Humanity was created in 1976 and is now a global presence, with headquarters in Americus. The principle is simple: if you want a home, put in three hundred hours of your own work, and we will provide free labor and free materials through our network of volunteers. Habitat homes have been built in seventy-nine countries and in all of the fifty states of the USA. Each house construction begins with a service of dedication, and a Bible is handed over with the keys; the work is an act of worship, which brings to the new owner a real attachment to his house as a sign of God's grace in the world. Not surprisingly, Habitat for Humanity is one of the most successful low-income developers in the world, though one whose profits are all ploughed back into its next generation of beneficiaries.

Millard had begun his business career in a state of obsessive pride in his achievements. While the money accumulated, happiness and inspiration waned. Millard's success was illusory, a form of stagnation that had only today's possessions as its goal. But when Millard began to look with due humility on his own work and talents, wishing not to profit from them but to make a gift of them, his energies were released in a new and far more creative way. He enjoyed the help and support of his wife and family; he felt able to throw away the pursuit of profit and live instead for a godly ideal; he looked on the world as an open adventure and went out to meet it with his faculties engaged.

And success followed—success of a kind that had eluded his relentless and self-centered business ventures of earlier days.

Millard Fuller was guided by his Christian faith; and humility has often been singled out as the Christian virtue *par excellence*: the virtue of Christ himself, who humbled himself before all humanity in order to offer salvation through a humiliating death. Yet humility has been prized too by Hindus, Buddhists, Muslims and Jews, all of whom recognize the need of humanity to humble itself before God, and to prepare constantly to exchange worldly ambition for a life of meekness and prayer. The life in humility has shaped the monastic communities of Europe and Asia, and is followed too by the Sufi mystics and by Tibet's exiled Dalai Lama. These unworldly people secretly benefit the rest of us, for they are in the business of accumulating the spiritual capital on which we depend in our times of need. In the case of Millard Fuller, we see how a man could reach for that capital in his hour of desperation and discover life anew, so as to release the creative energy that was to change the world.

Humility is never more necessary than when you are dealing with people who need your help, where the temptation is to look down on them or to produce help in the form of peremptory commands. As all who have had to look after frail or sick people know, this temptation can sometimes be resisted only through forcibly reminding oneself of one's own eventual helplessness. In no predicament is faith a more vital support or a more welcome part of the daily round. We witness this in three strikingly successful faith-inspired companies: one, Sunrise Senior Living, which provides facilities for those entering their twilight years; another, Providence Healthcare, offering hospitals and medical treatment; and the last, CNL, which has become one of the world's largest real estate companies.

Sunrise Senior Living was founded twenty years ago by Paul and Terry Klaassen, strongly committed Christians in the Reformed

Church tradition, whose aim has been to provide seniors with a vision of their own future and a sense that life is at every age what you make of it. Their communities are designed to serve their residents, to facilitate choices, to recognize the individuality and uniqueness of each resident and to nurture the spirit. Friends and family are involved in all its activities, and residents are treated with respect, as people every bit as important now as they ever were. The most important virtue in the running of these communities is therefore humility: the ability to recognize in the frail and dependent person before you someone who is still, in the eyes of God, your equal, with strengths and achievements that might put you to shame. There is no doubt that humility, displayed on this daily basis and fortified by faith, has contributed to the success of Sunrise Senior Living, which now has more than 440 communities in the United States, Canada, Britain and Germany, with a combined resident capacity of more than 52,000.

Providence Healthcare is likewise governed by a spirit of humble service. This Vancouver-based company declares itself to be inspired by the healing mission of Jesus, following his example of compassionate care. It aims not merely to heal the body but to engage the soul, recognizing the God-given creativity, love and compassion that dwell within each person and which can be brought into the healing process. Providence makes active spiritual care teams available at all its hospitals, offering their support to patients, residents, staff and families. The staff are exhorted to be wholly accountable to each other and to the patients and their families. Every hospital contains prayer spaces, a chapel or place of meditation, and weekly reflections are distributed to the staff, designed to express the compassionate spirit of Jesus while being open to interpretation in the terms of other faiths. Although a Catholic foundation that draws on the work of the Sisters of Charity and similar orders, Providence offers its services to people of all faiths and of none. The important goal is not to proselytize but to nurture spirituality by recognizing the uniqueness of each patient who comes into care. "Living the Mission" sessions are held each summer so that staff can renew their commitment, and the hospitals are run entirely as though the patients are to be served and never commanded. Again, this spirit of humility has contributed to the success of Providence, which is one of the foremost health care providers in British Columbia.

CNL is one of the largest privately held real estate investment and development companies in the United States. Founded in 1973, CNL formed its first public partnership in 1985. It is actually not a single company but rather a community of companies in varying stages of maturity and independence. These companies are involved in a range of areas including industrial property, office buildings, REITs, retirement properties, hotels and resorts, restaurants, leasing, community development, banking and securities. CNL adheres to a conservative investment philosophy, valuing the quality of its assets over the number of transactions. The company describes its two most important objectives as "preserving capital and producing steady income for the long term." Its stated mission is "to be the most trusted provider of development, advisory and real estate services to our clients, while generating long-term benefits for our shareholders."

At the same time, CNL encourages its associates to maintain a healthy balance between work, family and community, and to make a difference in the neighborhoods where they live and work. Associates serve on numerous civic and nonprofit boards, and volunteer in religious and nonprofit organizations that are revitalizing the community where CNL is headquartered in Orlando, Florida. They reach out to schoolchildren through mentoring programs, particularly in poor and minority areas. An annual Workplace Giving Campaign benefits more than a hundred nonprofit organizations, with matching funds contributed by the company.

The chairman and CEO, James Seneff, embodies the spirit of the company that he and his associates have built. He is a strongly committed Christian whose spiritual bearings color everything he does and shape the mission and values of his company. In short, those values are: "Respect the dignity of every individual. Honor truth. Value our tradition to serve. Champion a long-term perspective. Develop people and foster teamwork. Encourage faithful stewardship." These values, while common to all persons, are rooted in a Judeo-Christian heritage. As a business, CNL has established organizing principles that guide its operational and strategic moves, including: a focus on underserved and undercapitalized markets, protection of the downside, the 80/20 principle, a contrarian nature, investigation before investing, a belief that relationships go beyond transactions, and putting quality over quantity.

Gratitude in Business

To many people, gratitude suggests a lack of power: if I am grateful for something, it is because it has been given to me, and to that extent I am dependent on the giver. Hence gratitude forms no part of the business personality as the Nietzscheans and the Randians conceive it. Standing on your own two feet means "being beholden to no one."

But we should see gratitude in the whole context of a life, and ask ourselves how that life is changed and empowered by it. There are certainly people who, after receiving gifts, resent the giver as someone more powerful than themselves. Soon, like Mr. Boffin in *Our Mutual Friend*, they begin to demand their habitual gifts as a "right," and to complain of an injustice whenever the gift is withheld. This we have seen abundantly with the rise of the welfare state and the ever-increasing demands made on it by people who have become addicted to its fruits. Here is gift without gratitude, and gift without the spirit of giving.

But that is an abnormal—indeed, a perverted—example of gift. In the normal case, the response to a gift is not resentment but gratitude, by which is meant a "going out" to meet the giver, a reciprocal offering of the self and its fund of goodwill. We are not demeaned by gratitude but raised by it to a condition of equality with the giver. We are saying to the one who bestows a gift on us, "I too would give, if I could, and meanwhile I give what I can to you." In the context of business, such an attitude, far from displaying weakness, is a source of strength: it fosters an open and honest approach to others—whether allies or competitors—and imbues the day-to-day operation of a business with a lightness and cheerfulness that help to release the potential of the workforce.

An instance worth considering is that of Truett Cathy, CEO of Chick-fil-A, the restaurant chain that Cathy founded in 1967, having started his own restaurant business in 1946 with $4,000 in savings and a $6,000 loan. Truett Cathy has remained faithful to the Southern Baptist tradition in which he was raised, and his corporation's statement of purpose reflects this faith: "To glorify God by being a faithful steward of all that is entrusted to us. To have a positive influence on all who come in contact with Chick-fil-A." Cathy has built up a billion-dollar business that now has 1,200 restaurants in a fiercely competitive market; yet he has achieved this while doing something that, in the eyes of the competition, is tantamount to tying his hands behind his back: he has insisted that all his restaurants remain closed on Sundays, so losing 15 percent of the selling week, and the day when parents are most inclined to take the children out for a meal. His motive is not just faith, though he adheres strictly to the biblical imperative of keeping the Sabbath. His motive is gratitude—the need to give back to God some part of his life, in recognition of the blessings that he has received.

As his business grew, Cathy became more and more interested in this need to "give back." He encouraged his branch managers to support their local schools, and instituted a scheme to provide scholarships to his employees; to date he has paid out $20 million under this program. And, through his lifelong voluntary work as a Sunday school teacher, Cathy has become increasingly concerned about the need to help children and adolescents develop as upright and responsible citizens. He has established and funded fourteen foster homes for children—the WinShape homes—together with other WinShape projects, such as camps and retreats, and an ongoing relationship with Berry College, in order to give young people the support and guidance they need. In his book *It's Better to Build Boys than Mend Men*, Cathy explains his philosophy, arguing that to instill good habits in the young is our duty, and also something that we can easily achieve through love and example.

Some might dismiss Cathy as a naïve product of the American South and its Bible Belt, with a philosophy that makes sense only in the peculiar circumstances there prevailing. In fact, his educational work shows an acute appreciation of the role of virtue in enabling us not just to manage our own lives, but also to achieve creative relationships with others. Aristotle argued that "we enter the palace of reason through the courtyard of habit"—in other words, that virtue is acquired by habit, and the habit must be instilled in youth. The virtue of gratitude, which Cathy displays, is one that was instilled in him during childhood, and which he took with him through life. And his schemes to "pay back" what he has received are regarded in the same way—not as arbitrary explosions of generosity, but as ways of providing systematic support for virtuous habits in young people who will go on to honor God in their own lives, just as he has done in his.

What has this virtue to do with business success? Cathy's business rivals rejoice in the habit that has given them one day each week without his competition; and yet his business thrives and grows. The cause is surely obvious. Chick-fil-A is a corporation with a distinctive ethos; its employees imbibe this ethos and find their energy and commitment amplified by it. Put another way: gratitude permeates the firm and changes its whole corporate behavior. It does not matter that the firm rests for a day while its rivals labor; for when it returns to work it is with an eager spirit, one that infects the workers in the restaurants and the customers whom they serve.

Tom Cousins founded and for many decades ran a real estate development firm that helped to remake cities, most particularly Atlanta. His many famous landmark projects include CNN Center, the Omni Coliseum, Peachtree Tower, BOA Plaza, the Pinnacle Building, the Georgia World Congress Center and dozens more. He literally remade Atlanta in the 1970s and 1980s. General Sherman would not recognize it anymore!

More recently, Cousins helped revive and revitalize East Lake Golf Club, home course of the legendary golf great Bobby Jones. He hired the well-known golf course architect Rees Jones to redesign the worn-out course. Today it hosts the PGA's season-ending Tour Championship, with the largest purse in all of golf. But the golf club was only part of a much greater—some would say vast—revitalization of the entire East Lake neighborhood, which had been known as one of the most downtrodden parts of the city. Today it is almost completely transformed.

Cousins Properties, Tom's company, is one of the nation's leading diversified development companies. Its mission, like that of most businesses, is to maximize value for shareholders. Since 1987 it has performed admirably as a real estate investment trust (REIT). Originally founded in 1958, the company has a solid reputation for creative development and leadership within its industry.

Throughout the country, in office buildings, office parks, downtown mixed-use developments, malls, community shopping centers and residential communities, Cousins Properties has stood head and shoulders above the rest.

Why? It takes business acumen and success to build more than twenty million square feet of office space, more than twelve million square feet of retail space, and some thirty-odd single-family subdivisions. What drives Cousins is the Presbyterian worldview that motivates his decision-making. It colors nearly everything he does: from efficient work habits to altruistic generosity; and from building the creation to caring for those less fortunate. Cousins has articulated a firm foundation of virtue for personal and business behavior. He takes seriously the biblical command to build and keep, and he believes that being good is in your own self-interest; what goes around comes around. A moral life, in the long run, simply yields greater happiness. He also believes that evil and sin are a poison on the soul.

For Cousins, taking faith seriously leads to the utility of altruistic behavior. The Golden Rule asserts an identity between himself and all others, he argues; this identity makes him his brother's keeper. In the brotherhood of life, one runs a business *ultimately* to do well so you can do good for everyone. This principle is embodied in Cousins' charitable foundation, which dispenses grants to needy groups to address a host of pressing problems. At the same time, a commitment to market principles is, for Cousins, a profound expression of faith in God's will. Nature's law and the laws of commerce are both, after all, part of divine law. There is little that is preachy here, just a lived confession of godly business.

eHarmony is a rapidly growing, marriage-oriented matchmaking business. The Web-based company was founded in 2000 by Dr. Neil Clark Warren and his son-in-law, a former commercial real estate developer who serves as CEO, with $3 million from Fayez

Sarofim and a number of angel investors. Dr. Warren, a well-known evangelical Christian with strong ties to the conservative Christian community, initially promoted his business through James Dobson's *Focus on the Family* radio show. More recently, the company has distanced itself from that approach in order to broaden its market appeal. In the last few years, eHarmony has received very large venture capital backing from two West Coast companies, Sequoia Capital and Technology Crossover Ventures. This $110 million funded a branding and marketing process that has brought heavy advertising on television as well as the Internet.

eHarmony is geared to those looking for a long-term relationship, estimated at more than 20 percent of those who use dating services. An explicit goal of the company is to help reduce divorce rates in America, based on its research into successful marriages and the careful matching process it has established. eHarmony users are required to complete an extensive questionnaire bearing on personality and values. They are not allowed to browse through a catalogue of profiles to choose potential mates for themselves; instead, matches are delivered to them on the basis of compatibility in their profiles.

The services offered by eHarmony are consistent with the social values of Christianity; for example, it does not offer matchmaking services to those seeking same-sex partners. Among the users, 72 percent belong to a religious group and 21 percent define themselves as spiritual; the overwhelming majority are Christian. The company runs on spiritual values and is rooted in Christian tradition, but it also employs modern technology and scientific studies.

eHarmony now ranks as the Internet's number one paid matchmaking service as measured by marriages per match. Moreover, using peer-reviewed journals and professional papers, eHarmony has done control-group comparisons showing that over 90 percent of eHarmony couples have marriage quality scores higher on average than those who started relationships elsewhere. They are said to be twice as likely to have happy marriages. With more than eight million users and some six thousand marriages achieved, eHarmony has an impressive business model.

In this chapter I have considered four of the "soft" virtues, which to many people seem inimical to business, and I have tried to show, both through abstract argument and concrete example, how they contribute to business success. There are other soft virtues that I might have chosen—meekness, for example—but the point should now be clear. These virtues are not acquired because people see their business potential. They come from quite another source, being part of the spiritual capital that is most easily possessed through a life of faith.

6. Spiritual Capital in a Skeptical Age

The cold, the changed, perchance the dead anew,
The mourn'd, the loved, the lost—too many, yet how few.

Lord Byron

In this chapter I address three skeptical objections to the argument of this book. These objections are not fatal; on the contrary, by addressing them I will be able to make a clearer path towards my concluding thoughts about the role of spiritual entrepreneurship in the emerging global economy.

The three objections may be stated thus:

1. *From the cynic.* So you value faith as an economic benefit? In that case, where does God come in? What happens to the duty of obedience and the devotion to the things of the spirit for their own sake? Are you not merely instrumentalizing religion, making it into an economic benefit, like good connections with the mafia?

2. *From the Christian.* Did not Christ tell us that it is easier for a camel to pass through the eye of a needle than for a rich man to enter the Kingdom of Heaven? Hasn't our religious tradition placed its greatest emphasis precisely on the retreat from worldly success, the adoption of the ascetic way of life, the renunciation of all material benefits, the life of poverty and prayer? Who could deny that the greatest store of spiritual capital is contained in monasteries and all that has flowed from them? (Think of St. Thomas Aquinas, St. Francis, St. Teresa, Hildegard of Bingen, and a thousand others who have kept godliness safe from the corruptions of the world.)

3. *From the pragmatist.* We live in an increasingly secular age, and the global economy is pushing us further towards a secular view of things as we strive to reconcile the competing claims of rival faiths. Faith must be sidelined from business, and something else—

an ideology, for example—put in its place. So what then happens to the thing that you have called spiritual capital? Is it lost forever, or does it transmute into capital of another kind?

Each of these objections is really a family of objections, pointing to well-known places in the psyche where the tension between business and the good life comes to the fore. Different people will express their worries in different terms. For example, the Muslim will not emphasize the ascetic way of life as an ideal, but will nevertheless experience the same kind of tension between his faith and modern forms of business as the Christian feels. Modern banking and investment, the pursuit of global growth and the credit economy all seem to violate the Koranic injunction against *ribå*, usurious increase. For the Muslim too, it might seem to be forcing things, to say the least, to align profitable business so closely with the pious way of life. Hence there is work to do if my readers are to be persuaded that I have really put my finger on a neglected aspect of the emerging global economy.

Answering the Cynic

Many things that we pursue as ends in themselves are also means to other goals. Consider friendship: The person with friends has help in his time of need, consolation in despair and fellowship in rejoicing. In everything he attempts, he is better off than the friendless person, and all his burdens are more lightly borne. But this does not mean that he values his friend merely as a means to achieving his own selfish goals. On the contrary, he values his friend for the particular person he is, and without thought for the benefit. The benefit is real, but it arises "by an invisible hand," from actions with another intention.

Moreover, the person who treats another as a means to his own goals, however gently, with whatever compunction, is not treating the other as a friend. And if you do not treat someone as a friend, he ceases to be one. From this we can derive a striking conclusion: Friends are useful, so long as you do not make use of them! Treat someone as a friend, value him for what he is, and he will repay your friendship a thousandfold. Treat him as useful, however, and he will soon cease to be so.

In friendship, therefore, we see the way in which people build up a capital asset by aiming at something quite different from a capital asset. The capital accumulates precisely *because* it is not thought of as such. The same is true of the motive of virtue—and this lies at the heart of an ancient insight, that virtue and friendship are connected, and that only the virtuous have true friends (as opposed to companions and accomplices). Courage, as I have argued, is supremely useful. It is the characteristic that puts your goals within reach, and so helps you to attain them. But that is not the motive of courage. The courageous person is not simply motivated by what he wants: the coward too has that motive. The courageous person is motivated in another way. He sees his action from outside, as another would see it. And he is proud to act as he does; he feels that duty, honor and his standing in the world require him to take the risk. And it is precisely because he sees his action in this way, as the right thing to do regardless of consequences, that he obtains the reward.

In this way, I believe, we should reply to the cynic. The examples I have given concern sincerely religious people whose faith has helped them in their business and who have been rewarded for their virtues. This is not the justification for their faith, nor has it been their motive. On the contrary, it is precisely because faith motivates them to other and higher goals, turning their minds away from the thought of profit, that they have been able to unleash, in themselves and others, the store of spiritual capital that has brought profit as one of its first effects.

It is a failure to grasp this point that lies at the root of the left-wing suspicion of capitalism and the market economy. Neoclassical economics proceeds on the assumption that firms strive to maximize profit, and that the market is a system in which individual firms, each acting to maximize its profit, coordinate their actions and achieve equilibrium. But neoclassical economics does not examine, because it cannot, the actual motives of the people who compose those firms, or the precise way in which the profit motive arises within them. To the critics of capitalism, therefore, it has seemed as if the whole system were built on ruthless self-interest, and that if anybody paused for a moment to consider the sufferings of others, it was only to study how to make efficient use of them.

If we look back at the founder of classical economics, however, we find quite another picture. Adam Smith's image of competition in the marketplace was intended as an adjunct to his detailed description of human motivation in *The Theory of Moral Sentiments*, in which the pursuit of profit is tempered at every juncture by sympathy and benevolence, and by the posture of the "impartial spectator" which is forced on us by our moral nature. Human motives are never simple, Smith recognized. What is from one perspective the pursuit of profit might be, from another and equally valid perspective, a gesture of benevolence. Often we achieve our goals by ignoring them, and the most profitable of our actions might be those in which we turn our backs on profit and act for the sake of honor, kindness or compassion. This I have tried to show in the last chapter, and it is the kind of consideration that ought to lead us entirely to reject the caricature of capitalism that its critics love to reiterate. Private property, private initiative, private risk and private profit are indeed all essential attributes of the capitalist system. But these things are economically effective only against a background of norms and values and an inheritance of human, social and spiritual capital that enables them to call forth our energies.

Answering the Christian

This book has admittedly been written from a Christian perspective, although in recognition that the gift of faith has been granted in other forms and through other channels. I am keenly aware of the ascetic tradition in Christianity, and of Christ's own injunction, "Lay not up for yourselves treasures upon earth, where moth and rust doth corrupt, and where thieves break through and steal; but lay up for yourselves treasures in heaven." (Matthew 6:19.) This injunction has its equivalent in other religions— in the Buddhist path of self-denial, as well as the Sufi Muslim and Hasidic and Talmudic Jewish traditions. But it is felt acutely by a Christian, since it is addressed directly to him, as a personal command. Likewise, the chilling statement that it is easier for a camel to pass through the eye of a needle than for a rich man to enter the Kingdom of Heaven is apt to induce second thoughts in a Christian, when it comes to endorsing the pursuit of wealth.

But that, I think, is the point. This book has not been about the *pursuit* of wealth, but the *obtaining* of wealth. It has been about the pursuit and valuing of other things, and about wealth as their worldly byproduct—a byproduct to be used to express one's gratitude and to do good here below on this earth. Christ's image of the camel and the needle's eye reminds us that to enter the kingdom of heaven we must die, and that when we die we leave our riches behind. The image, so chilling at first, is in fact a reminder of a truth that we must all bear in mind: which is that the place for wealth is here below, and it is how we use it that matters in the eyes of God.

Similarly, the injunction not to lay up treasures upon earth can be interpreted in the spirit of this book. Christ is attacking the obsession with profit and accumulation, an obsession that obscures the fact that our principal treasures lie within ourselves; they are the virtues through which we win our place among our fellows, and also our place in the hereafter. So long as we pursue those moral qualities, we can surely enjoy their fruits. And if wealth is one of those fruits, then that too can be enjoyed—provided that we enjoy it in the right way, not hoarding it in miserly fashion or valuing it beyond its utility as a means to generous action, but showing our grateful recognition of the gift.

The argument of this book has emphasized the way in which human achievement arises from and depends upon resources that are not mentioned in the standard inventory of material goods. These resources accumulate in surprising places, and in our Christian tradition no place has been more important than the monasteries in providing—through the discipline of prayer, study and devotion—the image of God's love and redeeming presence. And around that image our spiritual capital has accumulated. My point throughout has been to emphasize that material wealth is not the sole or the principal input into wealth creation; if it were, then the process of wealth creation could never begin. The primary input is human freedom, and the store of trust, faith and hope that enables people to work together to produce what they collectively need. The Christian call to the higher life, the life of self-denial, is a functional part of entrepreneurship as I conceive it. This is a call that can be heeded in many ways, once we see what it truly means—which is that our destiny is not here below and that our time on earth is a time of pilgrimage. Faith, I have argued, can feed into enterprise without polluting its own pure source, and it brings along qualities of character that make a success of business, just as they promote success in all other spheres.

Answering the Pragmatist

It is of course true, as the pragmatist reminds us, that we live in a secular age. There are plenty of successful businesses run by people without religious faith, and in any case there are many faiths in the global economy and success is not the monopoly of any of them. Why, in these circumstances, single out the spiritual input to economic success, when so many other inputs seem to be equally or more significant?

In reply we should take note of two important facts. First, an enterprise may be powered by an investment made generations ago, although its present leadership would never have been able to make such an investment for themselves. When Robert Wood Johnson founded Johnson & Johnson in 1886, he dedicated the firm to the cause of human health, laying down obligations that would put the customer first and the stockholder last, the whole to be governed by fairness and the grace of God. When his son made the credo of the firm explicit in 1943, it was in an orderly set of propositions, once again putting the stockholders at the bottom of the list of those to whom responsibility was owed, and invoking God's help in conclusion. This credo, which is constantly reproduced in business schools, is marked by American optimism, American public spirit and—most of all—American piety, which banishes the doubts that such a credo might otherwise raise in the minds of investor and employee alike. Over the postwar decades, the appeal to God's grace may have resonated less and less with the leadership of Johnson & Johnson. But it is what helped to install in the institution the attitude of experiment and social obligation for which the firm is known—the attitude summed up in R. W. Johnson Jr.'s much-repeated statement that "failure is our most important product." The truth contained in this statement is precisely what explains the fact that Johnson & Johnson has never posted a loss in its entire 120-year history. In other words, a corporation can be living on spiritual capital even when its current leadership may not see their lives or their business in spiritual terms. For corporations are persons, with souls of their own, and they are what they are today because of what they were in the past.

This spiritual inheritance came very much to the fore in the late 1980s when seven people in Chicago died after taking Tylenol (J&J's most popular product) that had been laced with cyanide. Immediately the executives of J&J withdrew all Tylenol from the market and assigned 2,500 personnel to an all-out effort to alert the public, despite the fact that the reported cases were confined to the Chicago area and were evidently the result of local tampering. This willingness to do what is right, regardless of cost (the cost amounting, in this case, to $100 million), is the legacy of the spiritual investment made over a century. And it contributed to the restoration of public confidence that enabled J&J quickly to re-establish its position in the market.

But there is a second fact of which we should take due notice, which is that spiritual capital may exist even in times when it is no longer recognized as such. A striking example of this is provided by modern China. For centuries, Chinese society was built upon Confucian values, acknowledging piety, obedience and respect as the primary virtues, and maintaining a vast web of communications and economic relations on the basis of a shared sense of what could and could not be done. Confucianism was dismissed by Mao, who set out to destroy Chinese culture and to trample on all pieties, in order to assert absolute and tyrannical control over the country. He ruined the economy, murdered millions of people, and sowed wherever he could the seeds of hatred and distrust. Yet the spiritual capital invested by Confucius and his followers continued to bear fruit among the offshore Chinese communities which had escaped the communist yoke; it also remained ambient in the souls of the ordinary Chinese, and has now begun to bear fruit in mainland China too, as resources left untapped for sixty years are once again exploited.

We should not think, therefore, that spiritual capital simply disappears when society is secularized and faiths compete. It is present in the institutions, the laws, the habits, the minds and hearts of people, even when they do not recognize its provenance, and even when they are skeptical of religious claims. What distinguishes spiritual entrepreneurship from other kinds of entrepreneurship is its conscious decision to make use of that capital by putting the glory of God firmly on the business agenda. It is a plausible conjecture that spiritual entrepreneurship renews spiritual capital; other kinds merely exploit it. But its presence makes a significant difference to business, even among those who are unaware that it is there.

An example is provided by Wal-Mart, the world's largest business today, and probably the greatest business success story of modern times. Of course, Wal-Mart is very controversial—anything that big is bound to be. But it is controversial precisely because it has brought into focus a tension that exists in secular values, and which secular thinking is not competent to resolve. Wal-Mart inherited from its founder, Sam Walton, an ethic of service: to provide what people want, in the way they want it, at a price they can afford. All other purposes were to be subordinate to this one, which was to be pursued in a spirit of ethical righteousness. Employees (of whom there are today some 1.5 million worldwide) are all trained to see their work as vindicated not only by profitability, but more particularly by the intrinsic goodness of providing what people want at a price they can afford. And this ethical approach has been emphasized by Don Soderquist, the recent chairman, who in retirement established his own school of business ethics with a view to propagating the idea of business as an ethical venture.

But Wal-Mart has been singled out by environmentalists, New Urbanists and left-communitarians as a public enemy, the cause of social decay and environmental destruction wherever it alights. The charge is that Wal-Mart, by taking advantage of the cheaper rents and easier zoning restrictions on the edge of a town, can effortlessly undercut the downtown stores that have served to keep the center alive over the years, and that Wal-Mart, by driving those stores out of business, kills off the town, increases dependence on motor transport, cultivates an "edge city," and makes its own special contribution to uglification in the plaza where it is dumped.

These charges may be highly exaggerated, but they bring into focus a real tension in secular values—between the ethic of service, which tells us to give to others what they want, and the ethic of community, which tells us to create the kind of environment in which people can mingle and build up relations of interest and mutual dependence through the atmosphere of a shared settlement. This tension infects the market economy at every level in a secular society, and is responsible for some of the criticism fired at capitalism from the left. Capitalism is constantly described on the left as the solvent of community, the anarchic force that blows like a storm across every form of human settlement, uprooting and displacing, making people strangers to each other, by putting consumer demand before communal affection. And radical leftists are not likely to be mollified by the "cult-like culture," as so many have described it, of Wal-Mart itself, which can bring to mind, when shown in a hostile light, the stupefying rituals of Huxley's *Brave New World*. To call this ethical business, the leftist will say, is to confuse real moral order with degrading kitsch. To that accusation others may be added: notably, the strong warnings against suburbanization and unsustainable sprawl, powerfully expressed by urban planners, and the equally strong warnings against the loss of social capital that ensues, as the endless solitude of suburbia settles like a mist over the American soul.

We can clarify the argument by suggesting that values are of two radically different kinds: individual and shared. A shared value is something that is good for a group of people and not just good for each individual member of the group; and part of its being good consists in the understanding that it is held in common. The goods of community are like this: one thing we value in them is that others value them too. It is in such a way that we value our urban fabric, our parks, our festivals and the other marks of human settlement. And these shared values are in tension with the individual values represented by each person's shopping list. By ministering primarily to the second, a firm like Wal-Mart jeopardizes the first; and this is the explanation for the hostility with which it is so often greeted.

The tension just touched on can be witnessed in every aspect of American and most of European modern life. People hunger for settled communities, lasting relationships, secure and homely environments—shared values in the fullest sense. But they are also adamant that they are sovereign over their own lives, entitled to pursue what they want, and they are glad of the person or firm that provides it. The communitarian movement in America arose from the perception that the old socialist solution to this paradox—which is state control of the economy—is merely another way of perpetuating it. Nevertheless, the communitarians wish to resolve the paradox in favor of secular society, by finding some way in which people can agree to restrain their appetites in the interests of what they find to be a genuine community.

Well, there is such a way. But it is not the way of secular society. It is the way of faith. Wal-Mart is the perfect exemplar of ethics somewhat divorced from faith, and is to be contrasted with those genuinely faith-based enterprises, such as Chick-fil-A, which put the local community and its needs at the heart of their thinking and make room for the renewal of spiritual capital. Chick-fil-A is not in the business of uprooting the downtown community or interfering with the rhythm on which it depends. Its attitude to Sunday working exemplifies its respect for the religious needs of real communities, and it offers people what they want while gently insisting that worship stands higher in the scheme of things than sandwiches. The settled community is a natural spinoff from Chick-fil-A's way of trading, and it is one reason why it does not attract the anger that is so often directed at Wal-Mart.

Yet while Chick-fil-A is in the business of renewing spiritual capital, it is also, like Wal-Mart, in the business of exploiting that capital. The very ability of Don Soderquist to present the Wal-Mart ideology as an ethical idea, and to mobilize the staff and the customers in support of that idea, is dependent upon a spiritual legacy, which emphasizes the essential nobility of human freedom and human wants. It is because Americans believe in the higher destiny of the human being, however described, that they can believe in the redemptive quality of an enterprise that sets out to give people just what they want. This is understood as helping people to grow and develop, furthering their freedom, increasing their control over their lives. And the origin of all these ideas lies in the religious inheritance that they covertly exercise.

There is another and more subtle way of responding to the pragmatist. In Chapter Three I discussed two cases—Elcoteq and Van Ede—of firms which, while eschewing commitment to any definite faith community, have nevertheless introduced a spiritual component into their working practices. Such firms are trying to create the space, as it were, in which their employees' faith can grow. And that faith may vary from employee to employee, and indeed will so vary in a secular age like ours. As Spirit at Work has shown, this form of spiritual enterprise is more common than is often imagined. And it is particularly suited to corporations that are either multinational or based in countries like India in which several different spiritual traditions coexist.

Exemplary of this new kind of spiritual enterprise is Aarti International Ltd., a cotton yarn spinning company that began in 1977 as the Aarti Group, with a small rolling mill in India. Aarti's core values stem from the Hindu spiritual tradition, which enjoins us to accept people as they are and to live in the present, bound to others in relations of love, compassion and mutual responsibility. Believing that work should be a form of worship and a means of personal growth, Aarti organizes the workplace as an open forum in which mutual trust emerges as the prevailing ethos. It provides group meditation programs, opportunities for reflection, and forms of community service in which the workforce can participate. At the same time, although working from Hindu premises, it cultivates an open, ecumenical and secular form of spirituality, enabling each employee to find his own spiritual niche, so to speak. It was for this reason that Aarti was granted the Spirit at Work award for 2004 and it is also the reason why Aarti has expanded to become a highly successful multinational, with $200 million of sales in the same year.

What we observe in an enterprise like Aarti is the *form* of spiritual enterprise, but without specific *content*. Aarti is helped in this by the eclectic nature of the Hindu tradition, many elements of which have been devoted precisely to defining and pursuing a kind of creedless spirituality, based purely on the conception of the self and the search for self-transcendence in the universal "I." This search, connected with the spiritual exercises of Yoga and with a kind of other-directed and duty-filled discipline, has made Hinduism especially adaptable to the demands of modern and skeptical people. And the evidence is that many firms are moving in this direction, in order to open up the channels through which spiritual capital can enter the business, while steering clear of all dogmatism concerning which channels are the right ones. It is surely reasonable to suppose that, in the global market to which all major enterprises are now turned, such an approach will increasingly be welcomed by employees and customers alike.

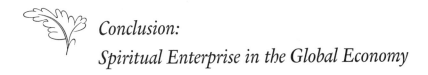

Conclusion:
Spiritual Enterprise in the Global Economy

After all there is but one race – humanity.

George Moore

Some sociologists, economists or pundits might object to the argument of this book in the following terms: What you have been describing (they might say) is really just a narrow aspect of social capital. Virtues are the habits through which we build up networks of trust. We can acquire them in many ways, and the way of faith is only one. What matters is that we do acquire them, and with them the networks that facilitate enterprise. There is no need here for a concept of spiritual capital as an additional input into the economic process. There is no such thing as spiritual enterprise.

To this objection I make the following reply: Social capital and the enterprises they sustain are built up through social interaction; virtue is a part of it, to the extent that virtue is encouraged by social mores, by the praise and criticism of one's fellows, and by the interactions whereby we learn the ways of trust. But spiritual capital, while it feeds into that process and provides it with an invaluable underpinning, is built up in another way. It comes from another relation altogether than the relations of human society: the relation with God. The reaching out towards God through worship, prayer, devotion and pious observance is a specific kind of discipline, which is not the discipline of human society. It involves an act of metaphysical submission, a bowing down of the whole spirit to a power that lies beyond the world of our perception. This posture of spiritual reception, whereby the individual opens his heart to an other-worldly form of obedience, is the core of piety, and it provides unique forms of practical knowledge—for example, the knowledge of what to do and how to behave in circumstances where the existing writ of social mores does not run, the knowledge of how to forgive someone who has tried to destroy you, the knowledge of how to ask forgiveness for your own recognized faults. It also begins with thankful praise and leads to humility and gratitude. As Max DePree once said, the first and last word of leadership is thanks. It both sets the direction and motivates.

The habit of prayer may be particularly important in this respect, and it is an aspect of Islamic communities that makes a vivid impression on their visitors. Regular prayer involves a constant renewal of the spirit, a never-ending realignment of one's imperfect nature with a divine archetype. And when it comes to serious choices, the ability to lay them before a person believed to be one's maker and one's judge is of unparalleled help in coming to a decision. Animals don't make decisions; they merely follow their desires. We rational beings, endowed with personality, freedom and accountability, are able to commit ourselves through our choices, and to call down judgment by making those choices our own. How much easier this momentous feature of the human condition becomes when we rehearse those choices in prayer.

People with faith believe that spiritual capital comes to them from God; that they renew it and accumulate it through "parleying with their maker," as Jonathan Ruffer put it. But agnostics and unbelievers are also able to recognize spiritual capital as a distinct input into economic life. For them it does not come from God, but from the individual's belief and trust in him, and from that reaching out towards the transcendental which—while it may never reach its target, since there is no target to be reached—creates the inner discipline of the soul that permits the transmission of this wholly special kind of practical knowledge. That there is this distinct kind of practical knowledge is something that I have tried to show through my examples. That it is brought to us by a higher power is an item of faith, and not of empirical observation. Even atheists, motivated by the "belief in belief" that Daniel Dennett (*Breaking the Spell*) identified as the after-image of religion, are able to see that spiritual capital is a much-needed and perhaps even irreplaceable input into a free economy.

I have tried to show the centrality of faith in the workings of business. The reader will almost certainly want to know how I envisage the future. How in particular does spiritual enterprise help us to seize the opportunities presented by the emerging global economy?

The global economy is nothing new. It existed in the days of Christ himself, protected and encouraged by the Roman Empire, and extending to the very limits of the known world. The spread of the Christian faith is itself a product of globalization, and the first moves towards a Christian theology are contained in letters sent by St. Paul to the far outposts of the empire. What is new is not so much the global economy but the speed with which ideas, information and assets can be transferred around the world. This speed has shrunk all distances to negligible proportions and has enabled firms in one part of the globe to compete openly with firms in another, whatever the distance between them. This fact presents new opportunities and new dangers. The opportunities are obvious: new markets, new partnerships, new forms of human life with which to stimulate the commercial imagination. The dangers are less evident, but equally real: the hostility provoked by insensitive marketing, by aggressive competition, by manners and images that are offensive to rooted values and religious beliefs and by products that are marketed regardless of their adverse side effects.

Americans more than others, because of their cheerful and forward-looking approach to things, sometimes blunder when encountering more melancholy and backward-looking people. They tend to be puzzled by the fact that people dislike the sight of McDonald's yellow arches on a medieval townhouse, utter the word "Disney" as a term of abuse, or denounce Monsanto as the enemy of the family farm. And the accumulated hostility can take radical forms, as we have seen from al-Qaeda, not to speak of the growing anti-Americanism in France, Germany and Spain.

The realistic response to this hostility is to grasp the opportunities while avoiding the dangers. We avoid the dangers by treating other people, competitors included, with respect, by emphasizing our shared humanity and our shared stewardship of the earth and its resources, and by acknowledging our common dependence on a Creator God. An example of considerable interest is provided by the celebrated investment manager Sir John Templeton, who was the first to create a global network of mutual funds.

Templeton began adult life with the ambition to become a minister, but while at Yale he came to the conclusion that he could best serve God and humanity by exploiting his gift for financial analysis. This gift is not simply a matter of advising clients how to obtain the best return on their investment. It has much more to do with wealth creation than with wealth distribution. Wise investment produces a return because it brings one person's savings into creative contact with another person's energy. Hence the successful financial analyst is also releasing the economic potential of people, by bringing the capital investment that they need. This means trusting them and inviting them to trust. Templeton expresses his vision in the thought that all people are "only the tiniest part of God." Hence "each of us should try to love every human being without *any* exceptions, and not just a little bit, but unlimited love for every human being with absolutely no exceptions."

This belief, which reflects Templeton's Christian faith, led him to the view that investment should be a global exercise, extending the opportunity to explore their creative potential to people everywhere, and especially to those who have been marginalized by the march of capitalist progress. Hence he founded an international approach to investing, looking for economic value in Asia and the Middle East, Australia and remote parts of Africa. Templeton did not see himself as a missionary at all and made no effort to convert the people in whose businesses he invested his clients' funds. It was sufficient for him that they were human beings, with their own spiritual and moral inheritance, who would respond to trust with trust. Templeton's business grew from a one-room operation above a local police station into a multibillion-dollar corporation, extensively involved in charitable and philanthropic work.

Templeton regarded his success in business as a gift from God, and one that demanded gratitude. Accordingly he has used his fortune to promote charitable causes, to relay to our secular world the knowledge of the spirit that inspired him, and to provide help and support to many whose talents are much needed but who find no easy way of supporting themselves in a skeptical culture. He illustrates the kind of giving that ought always to accompany commercial success, and which adds a human dimension to the global economy.

It is perhaps unnecessary to refer to Enron as an example of a global venture that has suffered the consequences of conducting business without cultivating virtue. But here it is significant that Enron's initial success was due to the faith-based attitude of Kenneth Lay, its CEO. Lay is the son of a Baptist minister, and a self-confessed "strong believer that one of the most satisfying things in life is to create a highly moral and ethical environment in which every individual is allowed and encouraged to realize their God-given potential." Lay's injecting of spiritual capital was neutralized and turned against itself as the firm began to pursue profit at any cost and without regard for the ethical principles professed by its chief executive.

It is perhaps equally unnecessary to refer to McDonald's as a global corporation that has become too vivid a symbol of Americanization to gain the full approbation of the places where it is now installed, and whose aesthetic, culinary and social mores it cannot avoid affecting. Lack of respect for local people and local cultures has jeopardized its business in France and made it a target of anger elsewhere. The refusal of its British branches to buy British beef just as soon as the BSE scare hit the headlines has led also to a strong reaction from British farmers. And its insistence on disfiguring the townscape with its childish logo has led to strong negative reactions in places like Italy and the Czech Republic, whose unspoiled architectural heritage is at risk from this kind of insensitive branding. The McDonald's name is now a byword for the unwanted aspects of the global economy among those who campaign against it. Of course, it is also a byword for instant gratification among the ordinary people who have never before enjoyed food of this kind, served in so friendly and open a manner. The opening of McDonald's Moscow store left Lenin's mausoleum without a visitor. Nevertheless, McDonald's has come to epitomize, in the mind of many Europeans at least, the ruthless morality of the "brand," and has thus catalyzed a wholly new kind of reaction against the global economy, in the wake of the highly acclaimed, if somewhat meretricious, attack on the insensitive branding of our world in *No Logo*.

The role of multinational business in transforming the cultural and spiritual landscape of Europe, Latin America, Asia, Africa and the Middle East has therefore now become a topic of intense interrogation, some laudatory, much hostile, and it is clear that there are few people around who would unreservedly praise all that has been done in the name of globalization. It is all the more necessary, therefore, to enter the global market from a secure spiritual and moral base in order not merely to maintain self-confidence, but also to engender trust wherever one ventures. It is precisely in this respect that spiritual enterprise can be of most service to business.

True spiritual enterprise is not a form of "window dressing," and it is a long way from the kind of "grafted on" public relations exercise that is known as "corporate social responsibility." Enron was quite good at CSR, giving money to fashionable causes, making the right noises about diversity, equal opportunity, care for the environment, and whatever else the activists were concerned to investigate. But CSR, conceived in this way, is simply a kind of protection racket, whereby a corporation buys off the busybodies among the NGOs, wraps itself in a veil of political correctness and gets on with the business of profit-taking. It is only superficially related to the ethical heart of a business, and may indeed be nothing more than a systematic deception—like the advertisements and PR for oil companies that present them as engaged almost exclusively in environmental programs and never mention fossil fuels, still less greenhouse gas emissions. This is not to say that oil companies should not be involved in environmental projects—of course they should. It is rather to emphasize the nature of the company as a responsible citizen, not a public relations façade.

The considerations that might make us suspicious of CSR ought also to weigh against the current orthodoxies of "business ethics," as it is now taught in business courses and MBA programs, and as it intrudes into the political sphere. "Business ethics" typically consists in a set of rules—dos and don'ts, calculated to secure the approval of "stakeholders" and therefore of the activists who claim to represent them. It is animated by a kind of political correctness, which itself stems from the same suspicion of the "profit motive" as do the socialist resentments that poisoned t he heart of Europe in the twentieth century. Diversity, multiculturalism, environmental rectitude and other agenda-driven prescriptions are made into absolute values, to be enforced without regard to the nature of the business or the conditions under which it can flourish. And business ethics, so conceived, prompts governments to devise ever more detailed regulations and to appoint ever more meddlesome committees of people—usually ignorant of or hostile to business—to enforce them. Of course, there is such a thing as business ethics; but it is no different from any other kind of ethics. It consists in one simple injunction: strive to do good. We obey this injunction through the exercise of virtue, and not through public relations exercises designed to appease politically motivated activists. Ethics is not about conformity to a political agenda; it is about the internal character, the moral stature, in short the soul of the firm. The virtuous company, building on spiritual capital, does not need to be told how to treat its employees, its customers or the environment; it knows from the outset that it is a steward of all that it touches, just as virtuous people are.

This returns me to a subject that I mentioned at the outset of my argument—the rise of the "stakeholder" model of the company. In discussions of business enterprises, the stakeholder is usually contrasted with the shareholder. The latter has risked his money in the firm, which is therefore bound to him by a fiduciary obligation not to waste or squander it. The former simply has a passing interest in the firm, whose obligation towards him is only that laid down by the general principles of morality and law. Sometimes a distinction is made between a narrow and a wide definition of "stakeholder." In the narrow sense, stakeholders are all those groups who are vital to the survival and success of the firm (employees, customers, suppliers and so on), while in the wider sense, stakeholders include any group that can affect or be affected by the firm. What should be a firm's attitude to stakeholders in the wider sense—including local communities, passersby and future generations, in addition to consumers, employees and suppliers, who are also bound to it by contract?

Some have seen the emphasis on the stakeholder as part of an attempt to align the capitalist enterprise with the principles of Kant's moral philosophy. In this view, care for the stakeholder is a moral duty, and the corporation is as much constrained by the categorical imperative as any individual. Even if that is true, however, it does not alter the fact that while the ordinary individual is not bound in everything he does by a single set of fiduciary duties, a corporation is bound by its duties to shareholders. Emphasis on the stakeholder should not be allowed to obscure the fundamental nature of the corporation as an association of individuals bound together by a shared risk and rewarded by a shared profit. The sharing of risk and profit creates relations of responsibility between management and workforce, owners and executives, and these endow the corporation with a soul of its own. Indeed, throughout this book we have been describing spiritual enterprise as a feature of a corporation's *soul*, and not just an exercise in public relations. Whatever the truth in the "stakeholder model," it must not be allowed to obscure this fundamental point: that corporations come into the world as distinct individuals, with souls that are shaped by the spiritual capital that has been invested in them.

Readers might be perplexed to see the word "soul" employed in this way. Surely, they will say, corporations don't have souls in the sense that persons have souls. There is no immortal essence to a corporation, nor does a corporation die and proceed to judgment. This talk of the corporate soul, they will say, is at best a metaphor. I reply that there are metaphors and there are metaphors. Some we can dispense with, others we live by. For example: we can dispense with "a sexy message," as all it means is a message that will appeal to general human interests. But we cannot so easily dispense with "a shining example," "a gentle melody" or "a loud color." Sometimes ("a high note," "a deep despair," "a troubled sky") a metaphor is essential to what we are trying to say. This is certainly true when we speak of the "soul" of a company. After all, companies do things, they are blamed and praised for things, and they deliberate, take responsibility and create bonds of loyalty and disaffection just as we do. When you belong to a company, you are acutely aware that it has its own way of proceeding, its own values, a corporate culture, and its own ambient consciousness of how to conduct itself in business. The soul of the company is simply a special case of *l'esprit de corps*, the shared sense of belonging, following, leading and obeying that unites the members around their common interests. Hence a company can be guided by faith, just as an individual can be. And this faith may make itself felt, even though many of the members do not personally share it, but employ it as one of the capital assets of the firm.

A company guided by faith will possess the virtues that I have described in this book: it will have the courage and perseverance to pursue its goals, and also the humility, compassion and forgiveness that will guard against arrogance and offensiveness. It will be accepted in the global economy not as a rapacious marauder but as a partner whose presence promises help, and which will conduct itself as a fellow citizen wherever it might be. Nothing is more valuable to a firm in the global economy than its reputation for virtue. It is not enough to be "visionary" in the sense now made familiar; a visionary company can easily offend through its messages or its aggressive presence, as Exxon offended the Czechs after the fall of communism by erecting gas stations surmounted by eye-catching and landscape-disfiguring tigers, or as Exxon offended just about everyone by attempting to evade responsibility for the 1989 Valdez oil spill. The need for virtuous conduct, rather than CSR, is nowhere more apparent than in the global marketplace. A company like UPS, which is perceived as a responsible citizen wherever it goes, has a clear trading advantage. But it cannot secure this advantage by window dressing. It must be led by a genuine ethos of concern and service—something that we see in UPS's involvement, for example, in educational projects in Poland that have radically increased its local standing, precisely because they are seen to be an expression of concern for the Polish people, rather than a mere exercise in CSR.

The increasingly central place occupied by China in the world economy has made the questions raised in this book especially relevant. There is a tendency among those whom Schopenhauer would describe as "unscrupulous optimists" to see China's move towards a capitalist economy as announcing the country's emergence as a normal member of the republic of nations. Such people overlook the fact that "capitalism" cannot be secured merely by allowing private property and private investment. There must also be rule of law and the kind of guarantees offered to the individual that will permit free experiment, the transfer of knowledge and the critical response to government. Those conditions do not exist in China, and corporations that are nevertheless entering the Chinese market are faced with crucial moral problems that, without the guidance of faith, may be hard or impossible to overcome. We have witnessed this in the case of two quintessentially postmodern companies, allegedly devoted to the pursuit of free opinion and open information: Google and Yahoo. The first has found itself acquiescing in censorship; the second has even become complicit in surrendering dissidents to punishment by the Chinese state. These cases show us the confusions encountered by companies operating on purely secular principles (however admirable those principles may be) when entering a sphere of genuine moral trial. The great tension that lies at the heart of the liberal order—the tension between free opinion and moral restraint—suddenly comes to the surface and, without the spiritual guidance that I have been advocating in this book, has a lamentable tendency to be resolved in favor of the tyrant.

Nor is that the only danger presented by the global economy. Global trade is riddled with much dishonesty, corruption and criminal malpractice. The emergence of the former communist kleptocracies into the market, without the deeply implanted legal structures that provide some guarantee of honest dealing, has radically changed the nature of global trade. Of the $39 billion in loans and aid offered to the former Soviet Union in the immediate wake of the communist collapse, $37 billion, it has been reported, was safely stowed in anonymous Swiss bank accounts within two weeks of the transfer. No accountant has been able to pass the accounts of the European Commission since its founding, and the corruption endemic to Mediterranean communities has been sent up through the European Union to set the terms of world trade.

It would be foolish for an American company, or any company with global pretensions, to ignore these facts or to pretend that the matter can be easily cured by transnational legislation. So what is to be done? Once again, it seems to me, spiritual enterprise provides an answer; maybe not the only answer, but one that enables a business to build on a rock in the ocean of treachery.

Consider the scandal of the *Savonita*, a merchant vessel that set sale from the port of Savona in Italy late in 1974, bound for the USA with a cargo of automobiles. Eight hours out of port, a fire broke out. The fire was extinguished, but a number of cars were discovered to have been damaged by water and smoke. The ship returned to Savona, where 301 allegedly damaged cars were unloaded and shortly afterwards declared to be a constructive total loss, and then sold to a dealer in Naples at 15 percent of their new value. The cars were insured with SIAT, an Italian marine insurance company, which had reinsured with Lloyd's through the broker Pearson Webb Springbett Reinsurance (PWS). Upon being asked to act on behalf of SIAT, Malcolm Pearson, the CEO of PWS, became suspicious of the claim. Investigations revealed that the reputedly damaged cars were being sold at 80 percent of their new value in Italy, and Pearson delayed pressing his client's claim through Lloyd's.

Pearson's dilemma was acute. He had a fiduciary duty to his client, to press the insurance claim. But should he press the underwriters to pay if he had grounds for thinking the claim to be fraudulent? Or should he recommend a commercial settlement to protect his future business with a big and important client? In the event, Pearson chose to resist the claim. He was sacked by the client and castigated by Lloyd's in a report evidently designed to exonerate the leadership of this once honest institution. Pearson found himself cast out from the world of marine insurance, with his business in tatters. Meanwhile, however, he had placed the relevant documentation with a member of the House of Commons, who raised the matter in the House. The press took an interest, and questions were raised concerning the conduct of Lloyd's—an institution which was soon to reveal its true colors in a spectacular crash that ruined the many innocent people who had entrusted their wealth to its keeping.

While all this was going on, Pearson underwent an operation for varicose veins in which he was immobilized, but for which he was given insufficient anesthetic. He was compelled to endure appalling pain as the veins were torn from his legs, and he watched and listened, immobilized and unable to cry out. Pearson entered a state of near delirium, in which a voice challenged him as to his belief in God. He found himself side by side with a companion, leading him down granite steps of pain, testing him, probing him.

> Suddenly I sensed that if I could end the dialogue, I could also escape from the pain. I had to get rid of my companion; I had to fight him off. At last I found the strength to be angry with him and I shouted at him: "There is no point in your going on with

me like this. I do believe in God. What does it matter to me if others don't? This pain does nothing to them and it isn't going to prove anything to me. So you can stop it. You cannot do any more to me." I heard my voice reverberate out in front of me and echo into the void.

Then stillness descended, and Pearson's companion revealed himself as a messenger, the kindest person he had ever met, who beckoned him forward into the darkness and through it into a vast space, limitless and full of light, where there was no pain.

> Time was a small part of what was there, but it was there. There was no conversation as I stood before the indescribable numinous presence. I stood in peace, felt part of it, and then knew I was part of it. I marvelled at the strength, and the justice, and the compassion. But soon I became aware of a pervading sadness too. . . . The sadness was there because we were losing, and we were losing because people have lost faith, because they compromise everything.

This experience changed Pearson's life. All the doubts that he had had concerning the *Savonita* affair were swept aside. It became clear to him that faith in God demands that we take his side; in everything we do there is a choice between good and evil, and business cannot be hived off from the rest of life and conducted purely as a self-seeking game. God's purposes could be furthered or thwarted in business, just as they could be furthered or thwarted in all other spheres. Later Pearson came into contact with Solzhenitsyn and came to share in the Russian writer's belief that the world had been surrendered to evil by those without faith. And he adopted the Russian's credo: if evil enters the world, let it not be through me.

By refusing to broker the *Savonita* claim, Pearson not only jeopardized his business; he exposed himself to a hate campaign in the financial center of London. Finding himself the target of calumnies, he was able to save himself only because a question in Parliament had ensured that the truth was finally known. In due course, firms in the domestic market began to give PWS credit for its CEO's honesty, and slowly the business lost in shipping was made up in business accruing from other trades. Pearson attributes his ability to survive this great test, and to remain in business despite attempts to ruin him, to his religious experience and to the absolute confidence that it gave him in the presence of a guiding hand.

This instance is an exceptional one, of course. Not all people come face to face with spiritual realities in quite so vivid a way, and faith-led businesses are not, as a rule, led into the kinds of conflict with crime and fraud that jeopardized Malcolm Pearson. On the other hand, the global economy is not run on nice and neat American lines; it is not subject to American law; its actors are not, for the most part, brought up in the simple pieties of small-town America; and its networks include many—forged in Sicily or Moscow or Riyadh, or even in London—in which families, mafias, Masonic lodges, sects, politicians and criminal gangs are the final brokers of every deal. In the emerging world economy it is vital to be aware that winning through will require courage, discipline, justice and wisdom—and indeed, all the other virtues that I have discussed in this book. And even if there is a short-term cost to doing business virtuously in the global economy, there is also a significant long-term benefit, both personal and commercial.

I do not deny that people, and companies, can be virtuous if they lack faith. But, as I argued in the last chapter, virtue endures and spreads because it is sustained by and through faith. The spiritual capital built up by previous generations can be borrowed and invested by others who do not have the faith to renew it, though at some point it surely must be renewed. This renewal of spiritual capital in the business sphere and its specific enterprises is what the faith-guided company achieves. In the new conditions created by the global economy, the information revolution and the growth of smart technologies, it is more than ever necessary for all companies to be guided by their rich spiritual inheritance, as spiritual enterprises. For only in so doing will they realize an incomparable source of the certainties that they will need in order to succeed in the highly competitive and interconnected international commerce that we have come to experience.

A Gallery of Virtuous Companies

Faith

William Pollard, Chairman, *ServiceMaster*

Faith comes from the Latin fides, *which means trust. In a practical sense, faith implies an allegiance to duty or loyalty to one's promises. In the spiritual sense, faith implies sincerity of intentions and a belief in and loyalty to God. Faith is the firm belief in something for which there is no proof, requiring complete trust. Faith is the wellspring of purposeful living.*

Bill Pollard lives out his faith in the marketplace. He joined ServiceMaster in 1977 and served as chief executive officer from 1983 to 1993, when company revenues grew from $234 million to $6.4 billion. ServiceMaster has more than twelve million customers in the United States and in forty-four other countries.

Under Mr. Pollard's leadership, ServiceMaster achieved an average annual return to its shareholders of 20 percent. According to Pollard, the reason behind the enormous growth and success of ServiceMaster is its commitment to honor God and develop its people. Bill Pollard has a deep, abiding faith that was formalized while he was a student at Wheaton College, solidified when he served as vice president of the school, and tangibly manifested in the marketplace during his tenure as CEO of ServiceMaster. His company mission, simply, is to honor God. Pollard has also been involved in a host of religious organizations and charities over a lifetime.

Honesty

Steven Reinemund, CEO (ret.), *PepsiCo*

Honesty is the fair and straightforward conduct that adheres to the facts. It reflects an uprightness of character and action, and implies a refusal to lie, steal or deceive. Honesty is at the heart of commerce and provides the infrastructure of social stability. Without this virtue, deception and falsehood would dominate the market.

Steve Reinemund leads a complex global entity and has made it more competitive using his Presbyterian values to shape decision-making. He joined PepsiCo in 1984 as senior vice president of operations at its Pizza Hut division, which he led as CEO from 1986 to 1992. Mr. Reinemund then became CEO of PepsiCo in 2001. He was directly responsible for PepsiCo's five operating units: Frito-Lay North America, Frito-Lay International, Pepsi-Cola North America, Pepsi-Cola International and Tropicana Products. Under his leadership, Frito-Lay sales grew on average 10 percent a year, achieving greater volume growth than any other major U.S. food company.

Steve Reinemund's approach to honest leadership led to his rise as CEO of PepsiCo. He stresses the importance of understanding one's priorities in life. Mr. Reinemund's beliefs and values are a cornerstone of his life and leadership style. His life is defined by principles and a personal faith in God, which provide the moral compass that guides his decisions. Consistency and fairness have been critical elements that reinforce his leadership style. Reinemund developed a values model that he applies to his life: "My success model is like a chair with four legs. In the center is God. Family, friends, community and work are the four legs."

Gratitude

Truett Cathy, CEO, *Chick-fil-A*

Gratitude is derived from Latin gratus, *which means grateful. Gratitude is evidenced by thankfulness. It is a sign of humility and maturity. Gratitude is one of the most powerful tools for creating joy, healing, contentment, spiritual growth and lasting relationships.*

An entrepreneur whose life exudes gratitude is Truett Cathy, founder of the Chick-fil-A restaurant chain. In 1946, Mr. Cathy opened his first restaurant with $4,000 in savings and a $6,000 loan. Today, Chick-fil-A is the third-largest quick-service chicken restaurant chain in the United States. Cathy started from zero and built a respected franchise where religious values form the core and guide behavior.

A devoutly religious man, Cathy has taught Sunday school classes to thirteen-year-old boys for the past fifty years. All of his 943 restaurants are closed on Sundays. This is how Cathy shows gratitude to God and allows his employees to attend church, then spend the day with their families. His willingness to give up 15 percent of the selling week does not hinder his ability to grow this unique and quality restaurant chain.

Perseverance

Sam Palmisano, CEO, *IBM*

Perseverance is the action or condition of steadfastness. God responds to the persistent prayers of His children; in Matthew 7:7 we are told that persistent prayers do not go unanswered. We are encouraged to keep asking, keep seeking and keep knocking. Perseverance is a virtue that displays itself in steady persistence.

Sam Palmisano became chairman of the board and CEO of IBM Corporation through perseverance. He held a number of key leadership positions since joining IBM in 1973: president and chief operating officer, senior vice president and group executive for IBM's Enterprise Systems Group, senior vice president and group executive for IBM Global Services and Personal Systems Group, president of the Integrated Systems Solutions Corporation, and senior managing director of operations for IBM Japan.

Mr. Palmisano implemented chairman Louis Gerstner's vision to keep the corporate behemoth as one company, rather than dismantle it. As Gerstner's protégé and successor, Sam Palmisano was responsible for IBM becoming the first company to receive more than three thousand patents in a year. Palmisano then persevered to reverse the very stratagem that made IBM a computing powerhouse—closed standards. While many mistrusted the early initiatives in open standards, IBM succeeded in the unthinkable by making a business out of selling components to other companies, including its rivals. What allows Palmisano to persevere? He is a deeply private person but is sustained by a strong Catholic faith that keeps him ever focused.

Compassion

Mel Gibson, CEO, *Icon Productions*

Compassion is derived from the Latin compati, *to sympathize, to bear or suffer. Compassion is a virtue and character trait that balances the health of societies. Jesus says that "a Samaritan, as he traveled, came to where the man was; and when he saw him, he took pity on him."*

Mel Columcille Gerard Gibson was born January 3, 1956, the sixth of eleven children. His father, Hutton, was a brakeman for New York Central Railroad. When Mel was eight, his father suffered a serious work accident and lost his job. After a three-year compensation battle, the Gibson family relocated to Australia, where Mel was educated at the University of New South Wales, in a devout Catholic setting.

In the midst of a successful acting career, Mel formed Icon Productions and signed a $42 million, four-picture deal with Warner Bros. It was Icon's production of *Braveheart* that made Mel the biggest star in Hollywood. But he bet his entire career on another single film project, dedicated to the Passion of Christ. The movie was not exactly mainstream, as all dialogue was in Latin and Aramaic with subtitles. Gibson financed the production with his own money. Still, nobody would touch the movie. So he created his own distribution and marketing strategy, and the movie generated well over $1 billion in worldwide sales. Compassion for the Passion.

Foregiveness

John Tyson, CEO, *Tyson Foods*

Based on the old English forgifan, *forgiveness means to give up resentments or claims to requital against an offender. Like all virtues, forgiveness can be misunderstood and misused. "Forgive and forget" can be interpreted as "Don't be angry and let it go." But the healing effect of forgiveness is not achieved by ignoring the injuries. Rather, forgiveness cleanses the spirit from the poison of hate and anger.*

John H. Tyson is chairman and CEO of Tyson Foods, the world's largest multi-protein producer. Tyson employs more than 120,000 people across the United States and Mexico. The company strives to live out its values: "to be an honorable and a faith-friendly company; to serve as stewards of the animals, land, and environment entrusted to us; to earn consistent and satisfactory profits for our shareholders and to invest in our people, products, and processes; to operate with integrity and trust in all we do; to honor God and be respectful of each other, our customers, and our stakeholders."

John Tyson communicates that all of those on payroll work on the same team. "We don't have employees, we have team members," he says. So when employees filed a class action lawsuit, John Tyson had to dig deep to forgive. The suit was brought on behalf of all persons legally authorized to be employed by Tyson Foods at fifteen of its facilities throughout the United States during a four-year period. Tyson leads a huge organization in the cutthroat world of agribusiness. He went through bankruptcy and learned to forgive based on his own personal experience.

Patience

Robert Price, CEO, *PriceSmart*

The virtue of patience comes from the Latin pati, *which means to suffer. Patience bears pains and trials calmly, without complaint. It is steadfast despite opposition or adversity. As we display patience in pursuit of our deepest destiny, we continue to grow. Patience is the wisdom behind persistence. Patience focuses efforts on what we can change while accepting what we cannot change.*

Robert Price founded PriceSmart, a warehouse retail business, along with his father, Sol, in 1993. PriceSmart sells high-quality merchandise at low prices to its members, while providing fair wages and benefits to its employees. This was the Prices' third retailing innovation. Sol Price had created the discount store industry in the United States with his opening of FedMart in 1954. Sol and Robert went on to develop the membership merchandising business with their Price Club stores in 1976. Today, membership merchandising generates over $70 billion in annual sales in the United States, and PriceSmart has brought the concept to international markets, operating 26 warehouse clubs in 12 countries and one U.S. territory and licensing 13 warehouses in China.

Launching PriceSmart, however, compelled Robert to learn the patience of Job, as the company faced bankruptcy and he lost his teenage son to a brain tumor. Sol and Robert Price have demonstrated amazing patience as they uphold their commitment to providing both quality and value for PriceSmart members. The patience they know comes from a Torah tradition and a close reading of God's dialogue with Job.

Humility

Millard and Linda Fuller, Founders, *Habitat for Humanity*

Humility comes from Latin humilis, *meaning low and humble. Humility is the first virtue in spiritual life. Every virtue that is not accompanied by humility will likely be destroyed by conceit and narcissism. Therefore, when God grants you a talent, pray that he may also give you humility so you will maintain it.*

Born in humble circumstances in Alabama, Millard Fuller became a self-made millionaire by the age of twenty-nine. But as his business prospered, his health and marriage suffered, and he felt that his integrity was compromised too. These crises led Millard and his wife, Linda, to renew their Christian commitment. They sold all their possessions, gave the money to the poor and began searching for a new focus for their energies. This search led them to initiate a ministry in housing. Eventually the Fuller family of six moved to Zaire to test their housing model in a developing nation. The success of their project in Zaire convinced them that this model could be applied worldwide. After returning to the United States, the Fullers created Habitat for Humanity International.

Habitat's economic philosophy is based on what Millard Fuller calls the "economics of Jesus." The no-profit, no-interest components of the program come from Exodus 22:25 in the Bible, which says that those lending money to the poor should not act as a creditor and charge interest. Habitat volunteers have built homes together with more than 175,000 needy families in 3,000 communities worldwide. More than 900,000 people now have safe, decent, affordable shelter because of Habitat for Humanity.

Courage

Tom Phillips, CEO, Phillips International

From Latin cor, courage *means the mental or moral strength to venture and persevere, to withstand danger and difficulty. Courage is progressively more necessary as life matures us. Jesus spoke on the virtue of courage and fearlessness: "Do not be afraid of those who kill the body but cannot kill the soul. Rather, be afraid of the One who can destroy both soul and body in hell." (Matthew 10:28)*

Thomas Phillips launched his publishing company with two newsletters, three employees and a $1,000 investment. From that courageous entrepreneurial startup in January 1974, the company has grown into one of the largest periodical publishers in the world. In June 1996, Phillips International passed the $1 billion mark in lifetime sales.

Tom Phillips began Phillips Publishing with a vision: to provide specialized information in an age of specialization. While most of the world was running in the direction of mass media, Tom Phillips knew that people were "drowning in information but starved for knowledge." He established the company as a newsletter business, seeing this medium as the most effective way to provide people with focused, "actionable information" that could improve their lives. Phillips started in his basement and built a billion-dollar publishing empire that is now heavily involved in political action and leadership training. He had the courage to take risks, as all entrepreneurs do.

Respect

Michael Volkema, Chairman, *Herman Miller*

Respect, from the Latin respectus, *refers to the act of looking back. To respect some-one means to regard with deference or esteem. Respectful behavior towards others comes from recognizing the inherent worth of people and their right to be treated with dignity and honor. True respect leads to admiration and affection.*

Michael Volkema is one of the most respected CEOs in America. His company, Herman Miller, has been ranked as the "Most Admired" company in the furniture industry in *Fortune* magazine's annual survey of American corporations for nineteen of the past twenty-one years. The company has also been named in *CRO* magazine's list of "100 Best Corporate Citizens" and has received the National Design Award from the Smithsonian Institution. Herman Miller's office furniture products, along with furniture management and strategic consulting services, generated more than $1.7 billion in 2006. With seven thousand employee-owners, Herman Miller operates in more than forty countries.

These successes and accolades speak to the resilient character of Mike Volkema and his team. Mike is a native of Columbus, Ohio, and was educated at Calvin College in Grand Rapids, Michigan. He currently serves as chairman of the board for Kids Hope USA. Mike focuses more on relationships than resumés, and prefers to be known for taking up his responsibilities as a husband, a father of three, and a follower of the risen Christ.

Generosity

John Templeton, Founder, *The Templeton Funds*

From the Latin generosus, *generosity is characterized by a noble or forbearing spirit, by a magnanimous heart and liberality in giving. Generosity is one of the best ways to show love and friendship.*

Born in rural Winchester, Tennessee, John Templeton is today known worldwide as a forward-thinking and progressive investor. Having made billions through his innovative approach to investing, Templeton has become one of the world's greatest philanthropists. But he once dreamed of a career in religious service, and his first major philanthropic endeavor, in 1972, was the establishment of the Templeton Prize for Progress in Religion. In 1987 he founded the John Templeton Foundation. That same year, Templeton was knighted by Queen Elizabeth II for his philanthropic activity, including his endowment of Templeton College, Oxford. After selling the Templeton Group of mutual funds in 1992, Sir John focused his talents on pioneering new ways to create value and stimulate progress through philanthropy.

Sir John's great goal in life is to unlock the vast potential of religion and to foster progress in religion. His commitment to expanding and deepening spiritual knowledge has resulted in the Templeton Prize as well as the Humility Theology Information Center and the Center of Theological Inquiry at Princeton Seminary. The John Templeton Foundation, with assets of nearly $4 billion, currently funds more than 150 projects, publications and award programs worldwide.

Discipline

Don Soderquist, former Chairman, *Wal-Mart*

Discipline comes from Latin disciplina, *which refers to teaching and learning. This is what molds and perfects the mental faculties or moral character, through the control gained by obedience. Discipline can be found in what is commonly referred to as John Wesley's Rule: Do all the good you can, by all the means you can, in all the ways you can, in all the places you can, at all the times you can, to all the people you can, as long as ever you can.*

Don Soderquist exhibited both discipline and biblical wisdom in running the biggest company in America during its glory days. Wal-Mart is a global retailer committed to growing its company by improving the standard of living for its customers and serving communities around the world. With $256 billion in sales, Wal-Mart employs more than 1.5 million people as associates. Don Soderquist joined Wal-Mart as executive vice president in 1980. He served in several other executive positions, and was appointed as vice chairman and chief operating officer in 1988. One of his responsibilities was to continue Sam Walton's legacy—to be the "keeper of culture" for Wal-Mart.

Don believes that ethics in business is not a luxury, but rather a necessity for organizational success. He also believes that senior leaders bear the responsibility for building an ethical organization. Don earned a BA in business administration from Wheaton College. He was awarded an honorary doctorate from Southwest Baptist University in 1989, and later from John Brown University and from Judson College. In 1996, he was inducted into the Retailing Hall of Fame.

APPENDIX TWO

The Numbers

Here are some comparative data. Initially it may appear that there is no clear pattern indicating outperformance (vs. comparable companies or the S&P 500 index) for a given set of "virtuous companies."

Let me restate our thesis, and look at the data that strategically support it. First, it is difficult to show empirically a statistically significant causal relationship between ethical corporate governance/managerial practices and stock performance. This is because it is not entirely possible to measure or quantify ethical business practices and record data-point observations consistently from company to company. It is also tough to have enough companies to argue for a representative sample. I think, however, that you can show selected examples of how ethical managerial practices correlate positively with stock price outperformance (vs. peer group or market). Advocating for causality probably requires qualitative rather than quantitative arguments, as I have stressed in this book. There is a lot of research on socially responsible investing that also sheds some light on this topic.

The data show that these virtuous companies did well as they did good, outperforming their competitors in many cases and the S&P index in most cases over the long run. So maybe virtue pays off in more than one way?

Nominal Return of Target Company

		Daily		Daily		Daily		Monthly	
Data points:		04/11/05		04/10/03		04/10/01		04/30/96	
Start date:		04/10/06		04/10/06		04/10/06		03/31/06	
End date:									
Period (Yrs):		1		3		5		10	
Company	Ticker	Px.Appr	Total Ret	Px.Appr	Total Ret	Px.Appr	Total Ret	Px.Appr	Total Ret
ServiceMaster Co.	SVM	-3.4%	-0.1%	26.0%	39.0%	24.7%	47.7%	39.5%	87.5%
ABM Industries, Inc.	ABM	-7.1%	-5.6%	30.3%	39.4%	16.2%	29.4%	124.7%	176.5%
S&P 500 Index	SPX	9.8%	11.8%	48.8%	56.9%	11.0%	20.8%	97.9%	132.2%
PepsiCo, Inc.	PEP	9.4%	11.4%	46.0%	53.4%	37.8%	48.7%	97.0%	127.8%
Coca-Cola Co.	KO	-0.9%	1.7%	0.1%	7.3%	-5.0%	5.3%	2.8%	20.1%
S&P 500 Index	SPX	9.8%	11.8%	48.8%	56.9%	11.0%	20.8%	97.9%	132.2%
International Business Machines Corp.	IBM	-4.8%	-3.8%	3.9%	6.6%	-17.1%	-13.9%	206.2%	229.2%
Hewlett-Packard Co.	HPQ	74.9%	76.0%	112.6%	121.7%	11.0%	19.9%	59.3%	80.0%
S&P 500 Index	SPX	9.8%	11.8%	48.8%	56.9%	11.0%	20.8%	97.9%	132.2%
Tyson Foods, Inc.	TSN	-20.2%	-19.4%	56.3%	61.4%	-3.1%	2.9%	-17.2%	-8.6%
Smithfield Foods, Inc.	SFD	-12.1%	-12.1%	52.1%	52.1%	54.2%	54.2%	297.8%	297.8%
S&P 500 Index	SPX	9.8%	11.8%	48.8%	56.9%	11.0%	20.8%	97.9%	132.2%

Company	Symbol								
PriceSmart	PSMT	5.5%	5.5%	-80.3%	-80.3%	-50.4%	-50.4%	-56.3%	-56.3%
Koninklijke Ahold NV (ADR)	AHO	-6.8%	-6.8%	-75.3%	-71.4%	110.9%	131.2%	-52.5%	-41.0%
Wal-Mart Stores, Inc.	WMT	-5.8%	-4.6%	-10.1%	-6.3%	-16.3%	-13.7%	295.7%	324.9%
S&P 500 Index	SPX	9.8%	11.8%	11.0%	20.8%	48.8%	56.9%	97.9%	132.2%
Wal-Mart Stores, Inc.	WMT	-5.8%	-4.6%	-10.1%	-6.3%	-16.3%	-13.7%	295.7%	324.9%
Costco Wholesale Corp.	COST	17.6%	18.7%	52.3%	55.3%	61.1%	64.2%	470.1%	481.1%
Target Corp.	TGT	3.8%	4.5%	44.0%	48.9%	62.1%	65.5%	553.5%	610.0%
S&P 500 Index	SPX	9.8%	11.8%	11.0%	20.8%	48.8%	56.9%	97.9%	132.2%
Franklin Resources, Inc.	BEN	41.3%	42.0%	133.0%	148.1%	178.5%	192.0%	393.8%	442.1%
Charles Schwab Corp.	SCHW	70.8%	72.0%	10.4%	13.5%	125.7%	130.2%	374.2%	395.2%
Merrill Lynch & Co., Inc.	MER	41.0%	42.9%	33.8%	43.0%	104.9%	112.8%	421.8%	495.1%
S&P 500 Index	SPX	9.8%	11.8%	11.0%	20.8%	48.8%	56.9%	97.9%	132.2%
Herman Miller	MLHR	-1.0%	0.0%	22.3%	27.6%	93.0%	98.4%	323.2%	357.6%
HNI Corp.	HNI	25.0%	26.5%	138.6%	158.1%	102.0%	110.4%	353.9%	429.1%
Steelcase, Inc.	SCS	25.7%	28.8%	49.6%	66.7%	108.7%	121.5%	N/A	N/A
S&P 500 Index	SPX	9.8%	11.8%	11.0%	20.8%	48.8%	56.9%	97.9%	132.2%

Acknowledgments

It started a number of years ago on a beautiful and balmy, tranquil spring day as we flew into the Bahamas and went through the gates of the private Lyford Cay Club. My heart raced as I was about to encounter the world's greatest investor for the first time. I was not there, as so many before me, to gain some useful perspective on the market or to discover which global companies to invest in. My conversation was even more profound. Over time, I was privileged to have many conversations and to embark on a friendship that turned into a *challenge*.

Sir John Templeton was a humble, yet penetrating soul. His gaze was truly like that of a sage, of a person both other-worldly and so infused with spiritual information that he exuded *joy*. He presented me with a direct yet simple challenge: to demonstrate how enterprises and the entrepreneurs who started them are guided by a spiritual force, itself rooted in faith. I took up the challenge, and with his generous support and my own endowment I founded the Spiritual Enterprise Institute. It is now a multidisciplinary business-academic center, dedicated to exploring and analyzing the modern phenomenon of spiritual entrepreneurship and spiritual capital in the context of globalization. It approaches its activities within a framework of virtues that—while explicitly held and applied—are defined broadly so as to accommodate the perspectives of all faith traditions. The Spiritual Enterprise Institute (SEI) has become a world-class, high-visibility center that is having a major impact on corporations and other organizations, as well as the broader world beyond commerce and academe.

Serving a catalytic role, SEI helps integrate the spiritual principles and practices of virtue and faith into the mission, values, planning and operations of businesses and institutions in the United States and worldwide. This impact is far-reaching since it is changing, for generations to come, the way corporations operate and transact business in the global marketplace for the betterment of man and the glory of God. One of the earmarks of the successful integration of spiritual entrepreneurship is a renewed freedom of religious expression in the workplace.

This work did not result from my own effort alone. I have been blessed in this life with loving parents, a dear and helpful wife, four wonderful children, many friends and colleagues, and a community of clients and supporters who have both believed and invested in me. For this I am eternally grateful, fully acknowledging that no man is an island, nor is he formed of his own being. We are works in progress and God has a purpose in it all.

Neither is a book entirely one's own product. It is shaped by the tides of the times and one's own background, experiences, and mentors. Having been reared in an observant home and raised in the cradle of faith, I was never outside of belief. My intellectual pedigree, interdisciplinary training and a life of real-world work led me to undertake this task. As an academic who early on became a "recovering academic," I was perhaps fortunate to leave the ivy tower to join the blood, sweat and tears of the active life. I have been involved in politics, investment banking, diplomacy, and for the last two decades as a strategist in the corporate world. From Davos to Aspen and all the resorts and retreats in between, I have had the good fortune to interact with CEOs keen on inventing the future. I have come to know them and their companies intimately, advising them while peering into their souls. They and the companies they lead are what this book is about.

I owe and need to recognize a sincere and large debt of thanks to Roger Scruton, who helped me in a thousand ways to ready this book. I also benefited from conversations with too many people to name or thank here, but to whom I nonetheless remain indebted. I must, however, single out Scott Massey, Nicholas Capaldi, Skip Weitzen, Ron Mahurin, and my editor, Roger Kimball, who were particularly valuable in framing this discussion and developing the shape of the argument.

A special word of gratitude must also be included for the Templeton Foundation. Their generosity abounds, not only in the capital to commence this work but in the friendship and nurture to sustain it. Jack Templeton, MD, now president of the foundation, and many of his talented staff—Arthur Schwartz, Charles Harper, Barnaby Marsh, Kimon Sargeant and Pamela Thompson—have become a network of collaborators for which I am truly appreciative and through which I have been enormously assisted.

I grew up singing old and *new* hymns. The hymn-sings I most recall include the likes of "Hide It under a Bushel, No," "Deep and Wide," and the eighteenth-century classics. For me, faith was and remains the ultimate purpose for living and serving. Each summer my family would travel from the heat and humidity of the inner city of Philadelphia to vacation at a camp in the Adirondack Mountains, on the aptly named Lake Pleasant. It was as calm and refreshing as a heavenly breeze. That is because it likely was. It was a religiously inspired but nondenominational setting. They called us *gospel volunteers*—as if we were free and roving ambassadors for Christ. I guess I still am. I recall my last summer there, when I served as a counselor. Every Sunday morning at chapel, high on a hill overlooking that ever-pleasant lake, we would march in carrying about a hundred different flags. They were from nearly every country around the globe—from America and Britain to Zimbabwe. As we paraded forward to the stage, the orchestra would play and the ebullient choir would sing in the loudest and most melodic voices I have ever heard: "Crown Him with Many Crowns. . . . *Thy praise and glory shall not fail for all eternity.*"

Theodore Roosevelt Malloch

Jupiter Island, Florida
May 2006

 NOTES

page

xi   Jagdish Bhagwati, *In Defense of Globalization* (New York: Oxford University Press, 2004).

xvii   Michael Novak, *Business as a Calling: Work and the Examined Life* (New York: Free Press, 1996), p. 119.

xix   On wealth creation, see the works of F. A. Hayek, many of which are based on earlier works of Ludwig von Mises.

xxi   On the requirements for development, see Hernando DeSoto, *The Mystery of Capital: Why Capitalism Triumphs in the West and Fails Everywhere Else* (New York: Basic Books, 2000).

3–4   James C. Collins and Jerry I. Porras, *Built to Last: Successful Habits of Visionary Companies* (New York: HarperCollins, 1997).

4   "A team of researchers ....": Howard Gardner, Mihaly Csikszentmihalyi and William Damon, *Good Work: When Excellence and Ethics Meet* (New York: Basic Books, 2002).

4   "Some go further ...": Mihaly Csikszentmihalyi, *Good Business: Leadership, Flow, and the Making of Meaning* (New York: Viking, 2003).

5   Robert Putnam on social capital: "Bowling Alone: America's Declining Social Capital," *Journal of Democracy* 6:1 (January 1995), p. 67; *Making Democracy Work: Civic Traditions in Modern Italy* (Princeton, New Jersey: Princeton University Press, 1993), p. 7; *Bowling Alone: The Collapse and Revival of American Community* (New York: Simon & Schuster, 2001).

5–6   Dan Cohen and Laurence Prusak, *In Good Company: How Social Capital Makes Organizations Work* (Cambridge, Massachusetts: Harvard Business School Press, 2001).

6   Francis Fukuyama, *Trust: The Social Virtues and the Creation of Prosperity* (New York: Free Press, 1996).

11   Theodore W. Schultz, "Investment in Human Capital," *American*

Economic Review 51:1 (March 1961), pp. 1–17.

11   "Some add personality ...": Gary S. Becker, *Human Capital: A Theoretical and Empirical Analysis with Special Reference to Education* (Chicago: University of Chicago Press, 1994).

11   "Still other management gurus ...": Richard D. Crawford, *In the Era of Human Capital: The Emergence of Talent, Intelligence and Knowledge as the World Economic Force and What It Means to Managers and Investors* (New York: HarperCollins, 1992).

11   Thomas O. Davenport, *Human Capital: What It Is and Why People Invest It* (San Francisco: Jossey-Bass, 1999).

11   "Two Nobel laureate economists ...": Gary S. Becker, *The Economic Approach to Human Behavior* (Chicago: University of Chicago Press, 1978); Robert W. Fogel, *The Fourth Great Awakening and the Future of Egalitarianism* (Chicago: University of Chicago Press, 2000).

13   William Damon, *The Moral Advantage: How to Succeed in Business by Doing the Right Thing* (New York: Berrett-Koehler Publishers, 2004).

14   Ian Mitroff and Elizabeth A. Denton, *A Spiritual Audit of Corporate America: A Hard Look at Spirituality, Religion, and Values in the Workplace* (San Francisco: Jossey-Bass, 1999).

14   Patricia Aburdene, *Megatrends 2010: The Rise of Conscious Capitalism* (Charlottesville, Virginia: Hampton Roads Publishing Company, 2005).

14   "Others see the rise ...": Peter B. Vaill, *Spirited Leading and Learning: Process Wisdom for a New Age* (San Francisco: Jossey-Bass, 1999).

16   "In a study of American elites ...": Robert Lerner, Althea K. Nagai and Stanley Rothman, *American Elites* (New Haven, Connecticut: Yale University Press, 1996).

18   Alasdair C. MacIntyre, *After Virtue: A Study in Moral Theory* (South Bend, Indiana: Notre Dame University Press, 1984).

19–20   "Aristotle saw virtue as constitutive of happiness ...": Richard Schoch, *The Secrets of Happiness: Three Thousand Years of Searching for the Good Life* (New York: Scribner, 2006). For a full treatment of *the pursuit of happiness* see: Theodore Roosevelt Malloch and Scott T. Massey, *Renewing American Culture: The Pursuit of Happiness* (Salem, Massachusetts: M & M Scrivener Press, 2006).

23   Abraham Kuyper, *Lectures in Calvinism* (Grand Rapids, Michigan: Wm. Eerdmans Publishing, 1943).

29   Ayn Rand, *The Virtue of Selfishness* (New York: Signet, 1964).

35   John M. Templeton Jr., MD, *Thrift and Generosity: The Joy of Giving* (Philadelphia: Templeton Press, 2004).

36   On virtue and the laws of economics, see also Elizabeth Anderson, *Value in Ethics and Economics* (Cambridge, Massachusetts: Harvard University Press, 1993).

42–43   On virtue in adversity, see Matt Ridley, *The Origins of Virtue: Human Instincts and the Evolution of Cooperation* (New York: Penguin, 1992).

50   C. William Pollard, *The Soul of the Firm* (Grand Rapids, Michigan: Zondervan/HarperBusiness, 1996).

51   "working of grace": Michael Novak, *Toward a Theology of the Corporation*, rev. ed. (Washington, D.C.: American Enterprise Institute, 1991).

70–71   McDonald Williams, "What came to me at that time …": William Damon, *The Moral Advantage*, pp. 120–21.

124   Naomi Klein, *No Logo* (Toronto: Picador, 2002).

126–27   On the "stakeholder" model, see Robert Phillips, *Stakeholder Theory and Organizational Ethics* (New York: Berrett-Koehler Publishers, 2003).

INDEX